Edward Doyle

Cagliostro

A Dramatic Poem in five Acts

Edward Doyle

Cagliostro
A Dramatic Poem in five Acts

ISBN/EAN: 9783337337452

Printed in Europe, USA, Canada, Australia, Japan

Cover: Foto ©Thomas Meinert / pixelio.de

More available books at **www.hansebooks.com**

A Dramatic Poem in Five Acts.

BY

Copyright, 1882.
By Edward Doyle, New York.

TO MARY AND ELIZABETH.

Dear Sisters, now the basket is replete,
Lead. Only for you, I fear, its fruit, leaves, flowers
Would be unculled; hence, 'tis not mine but ours.
Lead, that we lay it at our Country's feet,
Rich sandaled, with an angel's speed with sweet,
Bright hope to man. When darkening, pelting showers
Thundered upon me, you led me to bowers
Where the hail fell not, where the sun, hope, beat;
Without your hands now, — these which oft lead me
'Long Hudson's slope where zephyrs, as loose-crowned
With blossoms, tip-toe tread, or billowy bound
The trees, splashing their nuts down, — I would be
Most lonesome; not more so, if cast to ground,
And hence, to pick more fruit up hungrily.

PREFATORY NOTES.

I.

CAGLIOSTRO, the Familiar of Daniel Douglas Home, the High Priest of Modern Spiritism.

"Cagliostro was, without any exception, the most impudent quack of his day. The story of his life is one unbroken record of audacious swindling. He was thief, vagabond, and coiner. He professed to have the secret of the Elixir Vitæ, and the art of transmuting the baser metals into gold. As a thaumaturgist and theosopher he gave out that he could summon spirits. He was an accomplice in the famous plot of the Diamond Necklace, in connection with which Cardinal Rohan cut so ridiculous a figure. He was driven in disgrace from every country in Europe which he polluted with his presence; and at length, in 1795, closed a life of debauchery and fraud in a Roman prison." — *Blackwood's Magazine*, Feb. 1865.

Professor Alfred Russel Wallace tells us that Spiritualism teaches that death "effects no change in the spirit, morally or intellectually." Commenting on some caustic remarks of Professor Huxley, who would put spirits, old women, and curates in the same category, he says: "Many scientific men deny the spiritual source of the manifestations, on the ground that real, genuine spirits, might reasonably be expected not to indulge in the commonplace trivialities which do undoubtedly form the staple of ordinary spiritual communication. But surely Professor Huxley, as a naturalist and philosopher, would not admit this to be a reasonable expectation. Does he not hold the doctrine that there can be no effect, mental or physical, without an adequate cause? And that mental states, faculties, and idiosyncrasies, that are the result of gradual development and life-long — or even ancestral — habit, cannot be suddenly changed by any known or imaginable cause?

. . . .

"The noble teaching of Herbert Spencer, that men are best educated by being left to suffer the natural consequences of their actions, is the teaching of Spiritualism as regards the transition to another sphere of life." Therefore, on the authority of the most philosophical of spiritualists, it would be credulous in us to suppose that Cagliostro could have radically altered his propensities within so brief a period.

II.

At the end of act second Dr. Squigginson's clairvoyance is at fault, an incident suggested by the following in "Modern Mysteries Explained and Exposed," (Boston and London, 1855,) by Rev. A. Mahan, first president of Cleveland University. "The past fall and winter, nearly one year ago, our seer performed a mission in some of the western states. When in the city of Cleveland, (we were there at the time,) and while delivering a public lecture, he suddenly stopped, and for some minutes seemed to be in one of his favorite states of abstraction, or spiritual revery. On coming to himself, he remarked that he was deeply, painfully impressed with woman's rights. 'Will Horace Mann,' he exclaimed, 'lecture in this city, this winter? He will. Will his subject be Woman? It will.' Our seer then requested that portion of his audience who should hear Mr. Mann, to compare what he should now utter with what Mr. M. should utter on his arrival, and carefully mark the correspondence between them. He then delivered a very spirit-stirring paragraph, in which the audience was intensely interested. He professed to the audience that, during the revery referred to, he had had a *vision* of Mr. M.'s manuscript, and thus obtained the extract delivered. When our seer was through, a gentleman in the audience arose, and remarked that he also *was* impressed to say, that what the speaker had just uttered, as obtained through a vision of an unprinted manuscript, could be found, word for word, in a certain number of the *New York Tribune*; and that, if desired, he would produce the paper and read the paragraph to the audience. Our seer, of course, was taken all aback by such an announcement, and remarking that he did not read the newspapers, went on with his lecture. We state facts as they were published in the daily papers of that city, while our seer was there; and to our knowledge they have never been contradicted or explained by him or his friends. An individual who boarded at the same house with our seer, while he was in that city, remarked to us that Mr. Davis was, while there, to his personal knowledge, a diligent reader of the papers. On his arrival in that city, Mr. Mann remarked to us, that up to that time, he had regarded Mr. Davis as a sincere but self-deceived enthusiast; but that now he was compelled to regard him as a deliberate impostor; and that for the reason that not a single sentence contained in the extract could be found in his manuscript; that the former was a very condensed report of a lecture which he had previously delivered in the city of New York."

III.

THE PHYSICAL SAVIOR.

"The mother of 'The Thing,' as Mr. Howitt reverently termed it in the columns of the *Era*, was Mrs. N.; John M. Spear constructed the machine, and this lady engaged to endow it with perpetual motion. Spirits, she declared, had informed her that they 'would make of her a second Mary, and she would be a distinguished mother in Israel.' Although two children had already been born in an ordinary manner, she believed herself destined to bring a third into the world, which should owe its existence to no earthly father. This 'spirit babe' was to be the motive power of John M. Spear's machine. Mrs. N. became pregnant, Mr. Spear toiled industriously at the frame which was to contain the 'power,' and in due course finished his task. The machine was carried to High Rock in Lynn, Mass.,—a place made celebrated in American spiritual annals by more than one ridiculous, and at least one tragical event. The language of the 'New Era' became glowing. It was announced that an 'association of Electrizers' in the spirit-spheres were about to reveal to mankind 'the new motive power,' God's last, best gift to man. The 'Thing' once born, would 'revolutionize the world.' At length the hour drew nigh. Mrs. N. went down to High Rock. John M. Spear, the machine, and various attendants from earth and the spirit world, awaited her there. In presence of this devoted band the mystical delivery of the wondrous babe took place; in other words, 'the power was imparted to the machine.' It moved slightly. John M. Spear shouted for joy. The editor of the *Era* hastened back to his office, and indited an article, from which the following are extracts: 'We are prepared to announce to the world, 1st, that spirits have revealed a wholly new motive power, to take the place of all other motive powers. 2d, that this revelation has been embodied in a model machine, by human co-operation with the powers above. 3d, that results are, thus far, satisfactory to its warmest friends. "The Thing moves."'

"We have the birth of a new science, a new philosophy, and a new life. The time of deliverance has come at last, and henceforth the career of humanity is upward and onward — a mighty, a noble, a Godlike career. All the revelations of spiritualism heretofore, all the control of spirits over mortals, and the instruction and discipline they have given us, have only paved the way, as it were, for the advent of a great practical movement, such as the world little dreams of — though it has long deeply yearned for it, and agonized and groaned away its life because it did not come sooner. And this new motive power is to lead the way in the great speedily-coming Salvation. It is to be the physical savior of the race. The history of its inception, its various stages of progress, and its completion, will show the world a most beautiful and significant analogy to the advent of Jesus as the spiritual Savior of the race. . . . . Hence we much confidently assert that the advent of the science of all sciences, the philosophy of all philosophies, and the art of all arts, has now fairly commenced. The child is born, not long hence he will go alone. Then he will dispute in the temple of science, and then — ! ! '

"Breath failed the editor, and other fanatics took up the cry.

"The machine was hailed as the new creation, 'the philosopher's stone,' 'the act of all acts,' the greatest 'revelation of the age.' John M. Spear sat for a moment in the seventh heaven, and Mrs. N. already felt the halo of a Madonna encircling her brow."

IV.

EARTHLY IMMORTALITY.

. . . .

"Other insanities of the kind have since occurred. There were in America the Kiantone Movement, the Sacred Order of Huronists, the Cincinnati Patriarchs, and, worst of all, the Harmonial Society. Miss E. Hardinge describes this last, as one of the most extraordinary evidences of human folly, credulity, impudent assumption, and blasphemous pretension that the records of any movement can show. The society did not directly originate through spiritualism. On the contrary, it was simply a parasitical excrescence foisted upon the movement by interested persons. As in the case of Mountain Cove, the leading spirit was an ex-reverend. A certain T. E. Spencer, formerly pastor of a Methodist flock, planned, and, with the aid of his wife, carried out this infamous affair. A settlement styled Harmony Springs was formed in Benton County, Arkansas. All applications for membership Mr. Spencer submitted to his controlling angels. They displayed a worldliness of mind hardly to be expected from such elevated beings. Rich dupes were eagerly welcomed into the harmonial paradise; but its gates remained inexorably closed to the poor. Once admitted, the neophyte found his wealth melt with wonful rapidity. The Spencers, like Dives, clothed themselves in fine linen, and fared sumptuously every day. Their followers were enforced to content themselves with an extremely meagre vegetarian diet; the inducement to do so being the hope of earthly immortality; for the doctrines of the Harmonial Society were extremely curious. Many spirits, Mr. Spencer taught, perished with the body. Others languished for a short time after the separation, and then expired. Only human beings who followed the Spencerian system, could arrive at immortality, which immortality should be earthly. And an indispensable condition of the system was that its promulgator should have full control of the property of its dupes. In a year or two the bubble burst. Dark rumors issued from Harmony Springs. It appeared certain that, whether immortal or not, Spencer and his followers, male and female, were extremely immoral. Dissension, too, was rife among the community. For a time Mrs. Spencer quieted recusants by diatribes on the annihilation which awaited them, should they persist in their mutinous conduct. "Death," she remarked, "is the prying into things that are of the world, and acquisitiveness, and keeping anything to yourselves, and looking into things too much for your knowledge, and inquiring into things that the angels only hint at, and questioning what the angels say or do, and doubting much, *and fixing up separate dishes for yourselves.*" Despite this sublime philosophy, matters continued to grow worse. Several members determined to take legal measures for the recovery of their cash. On learning this, the Spencers gathered together what was left of the spoil and fled. They were pursued, arrested, tried, and sentenced to imprisonment. Of the large sums which had been embarked in the 'Harmonial Society,' scarcely a dollar remained."

V.

THE SAVIOR, NO DEATH.

"It is a sad story. Perhaps it would be well to seek to forget it; but, as you truly say, it may serve to warn others. God grant it should. I am unable to give you the exact date, but some time in 1853 a strange piece of news reached us. We heard that at the house of Mr. X., some little girls had become developed as writing mediums, and that Mr. X. himself had great powers over a table, through which messages were given. He was a teacher of music, and a good, truly pious man. (Oh! he was honest as we all were.) Well, out of curiosity, I went to see these things; and finding that the seances began with prayer, and that all the messages given were pure and good, I came home and asked my husband to investigate the matter. How many times since then he has said, 'it was you who led me into it.' These words were not said complainingly; for what right have any of us to complain? We all thought we were doing right, and even now, sir, I can only say that, if it were a delusion, I still believe God will pity us, for our object was to glorify him. My husband was a man of great intelligence, and, in proof of it, I need only say, that he had been Professor of Mathematics in the college here. At the time alluded to, however, he no longer taught. By a number of fortunate speculations he had acquired a large fortune, and we were living in ease and luxury. (I see you looking around my little room, sir; but it must have been the will of God, and that consoles me.) Mr. X. said his table was moved by our Savior, but now, in looking back, I wonder how we could be foolish enough to credit such a thing. We were told by the table (the words he used was the 'Saviour,' but this constant repetition of a holy name is so repulsive, that for the remainder of the narrative I substitute the table) that we must take Mr. X., his father and mother, etc., to reside in our house and share with them the fortune it had pleased God to give us. I said to my husband, let us give them a large sum of ready money instead, and ask them to live elsewhere; for their taste is not mine, and I could not be happy with them. My husband answered, the life of the one we worship was a life of self-abnegation, and we must in all things copy him. Overcome at once these worldly prejudices, and your sacrifices will prove your willingness to obey the master. Of course I consented; and seven additions were made to our household. Then began a life of utter recklessness as regards money. The table ordered us to purchase another carriage, and four new horses. We had nine servants in the house. Not only that; but the table ordered us to build a steamboat. Very expensive it was. Painters and decorators were set to work on the house in which we lived; and however rich and beautiful our furniture might be, the table made us replace it with newer and still more costly articles. 'All this, sir, was to be done that our mansion might be worthy to receive the One whom we foolishly believed came to it.' We were told too by the table that it was necessary everything should be made as ostentatious as possible, to attract the notice of the outside world. We did as we were ordered. We kept open house. The results were what might have been expected. People came and made a pretence of being convinced. Young men and women visited us, and the table ordered them to be married. When they consented, the necessary outfits were furnished at our expense. Not only that, sir, but as often as these couples had children, the children were sent to us to be brought up, and I well remember, that at one time we had eleven infants in the house. Mr. X., too, married, and his family went on increasing itself. At last, no less than thirty of us sat down regularly together. This continued for three or four years, until one day we discovered that our means were nearly all gone. The table told us to go to Paris, and he would provide for us there. We went, and my husband was bidden to speculate on the Bourse. He did so, and lost. Still we had faith. As there were now but a few in the family, we contrived to live on; heaven only knows how. I have been for days together without other food than a crust of dry bread and a glass of water. I must not forget to tell you, sir, that whilst in Geneva, we had been bidden to administer the Sacrament of the Lord's Supper, and that there were sometimes from three to four hundred communicants at table. A monk from Argovie, left the convent of which he was a superior, and renounced the Catholic religion to join us. You see, sir, we were not alone in our blindness. Even during our trials in Paris, our faith held firm. My husband often said, that the table had sent us there, and that he would not return to Geneva without its permission. At last we asked for that permission, and we were told we might return. Ah! it was then that we fully realized our position. We were poor; and those who had profited by our fortune whilst it lasted, were the first to turn their backs on us. I do wrong, sir, to tell you this, for it betokens a restless and complaining spirit, and I have no right to murmur. I had almost forgotten to relate that, amongst other wild fancies, the table bid us build a manufactory in France. We did so and the undertaking proved a total failure. The place was sold for one thousand francs; not a tenth of what it had cost. You are looking at that large engraving, and wonder, no doubt, how it comes to have a place in my humble home. Well, sir, during the height of our folly, Mr. X. was inspired with artistic ideas, but strange to say, could not give expression to them. A professional painter was engaged, therefore, Mr. X. described to him his vision. That large engraving is taken from the picture which represented X's. idea of the crucifixion. It is at the moment when our Lord says 'I thirst.' The original painting was sold at auction by our creditors, with our house and whatever else remained to us. No, sir, we have never seen Mr. X. from that day. He married my niece whilst we were all living together, and had four children by her. She was called by God, and X. has married again, and, I hear, never alludes to the past. Yes, he has been in Geneva, but he did not come to see us. I will tell you one little thing which has happened within the last three or four months. (The incident not being at all to the credit of X., I refrain from giving it.) The character of the narrator is well displayed by the self-rebuking manner in which her narrative terminated.

"Indeed, I am wicked, sir, to have told you such a thing as this! God forgive me! I ought to have been silent about it. Please, *please*, forget that I told it. I am a sinful old woman, and I bow my head in all humility to ask heaven's pardon for speaking such harsh words. Even in his wanderings, my husband (the unfortunate man is insane) never makes allusions to the past. Oh, I am perfectly convinced, sir, that it was not our connection with this affair which deprived him of reason. He began to work with his head very young, and mathematics fatigue the brain so. It is very, very hard not to have him with me, but he is at times beyond my control. Still I wish I could be allowed to have him here, and care for him. It is a sad story as you say, but we were all striving to obey the dictates of what we thought to be a high and holy power. I assure you some messages were very beautiful; quite superior to what Mr. X. could have given. Well, the day of life will soon terminate for us, and then we shall read the riddle. Speaking of those messages, I fear, sir, even when we believed ourselves most humble, there was a strong tinge of vanity in our thoughts, for we all, of course, believed ourselves the chosen of the Lord. I remember that, often, on seeing a funeral move past me, with its gloomy hearse and trappings of sorrow, I have said to myself exultingly, 'how happy it is that we shall have no such ordeal to endure; Ah! for the table had told us that, as the chosen of the Lord, we should none of us see death, but be translated bodily to his father's home. Remember, sir, that neither Mr. X. nor any other of those concerned, made, or sought to make money out of the affair. We were all of us honest in our convictions. We bear our crosses cheerfully, therefore, for I cannot but think that, although we may have erred, the Lord will repay us, since we erred out of love for him.— (*Lights and Shades of Spiritualism, Daniel Douglas Home.*)

VI.

To many readers, much of the prefatory matter, as I make no direct use of it afterward, may appear irrelevant; I have inserted it to show that the drama is no caricature. That I have not reflected merely the exceptional, could be proven by quotations from the principal spiritists, from Professor Wallace down to Mr. Henry Kiddle. In conclusion, I request lenity for oversights.

CAGLIOSTRO.

(13.)

CHARACTERS.

JUDGE GUILDERBURY, an Abraham or Jephthah.
COL. GEORGE GUILDERBURY, a Logical Materialist.
SALVATION PLOVER, General Willard's personator.
DR. EMPEDOCLES SQUIGGINSON, a Medium and Builder of the New Motor, the Physical Savior of the race.
ALFRED TEMPLETON, a Clergyman.
CAGLIOSTRO, the Inspirer of the New Motor and the Second Coming, and the Spirit of John Keats.
PATSY, an Unprogresssed Spirit, and the Bishop.
RALPH RAYMOND, a Cagliostro in flesh.
SMITH VAN DOOZER, a Philosopher.
MRS. WILLARD, the General's wife, who is offered up by the Judge, her father.
MATILDA SAUNDERSON, Mrs. Willard's Maid and Sister, and the Spirit of Emma.
MRS. STANHOPE SQUIGGINSON, a Second Adventist.
LILLA LAMB, The Mother of the New Messiah.
MRS. LAMB, Lilla's Mother, and a Disturbing Influence.
FOURACRES, ANDREW and POMPEY, Servants.

SCENES — Monument Park and Denver City.

CAGLIOSTRO.

ACT I.

SCENE — *Monument Park, the white peaks in the distance. In front of a colonnade the ground has been torn by the horses' hoofs, and on the left, near a steep descent, lies General Willara's body. The Colonel descends from the right, feels the General's pulse and breast, applies a pocket mirror to his mouth, pillows the head upon a stone, and with a handkerchief, covers the features.*

 Col. (*Stepping aside.*) When you would shout, "for heaven's sake drop the pen,
Take mental rest, air, exercise," as if
I were a horse to be turned out to die :
You saw me dead before you, ay, seemed anxious
To make the funeral march a double quick.
 Judge. (*Descending*) Dead ! How be otherwise ?
 Col.   Is silenced.
 Judge.   What ?
 Col. Is superseded ; last campaign is over.
 Judge. It cannot be, no, no ! Can God have blasted
His own right hand with which he drew our country
Up, as a drowning woman, from the maelstrom
Of civil war ? No, no ! nor could have lifted
Her miles, bright leagues, above dark whirls of carnage
To let her drop. sink deeper than before.
 Col. A God ? pshaw ! see ! (*Uncovers the features*).
 Judge. (*Bending over, then shuddering back*). Lord !
Willard ! warm, brains out !
Mouth purple, as noon-anguished morning glories
Over poor Emma's tombstone, — now his own !
 Col. (*After covering features*). Unable to restrain his horse from plunging
Into the chasm, he must have sprung off here.

Judge. Lord! what will Jane do? My dear child! I hear
Her falling, groaning, see her frothing, bleeding
As were her mouth a battle-axe's gash.
She must not die! — would let her die?
   Col.   No fear.
   Judge. No fear! Forget her screeching, mad, hair-rending
When Emma fell in, was the food of mud-fish?
At each heart-bursting booming of the cannon?
When breathless divers rose with hopeless hands
To catch a breath, and then went down again?
And when poor Emma, after the lightning smote
The lake and crusted it with lifeless fishes,
Arose, and was so eaten who could suffer
Her mother even a glimpse?
   Col. I know all this.
   Judge. Forget it not, nor that she was too blinded
With tears, sir, to behold her cloud, affliction,
Was shining with the coming Prince of Peace,
Or see him smiling in the wave with hand
Of light out to the groper in the dark, —
That, crazed, she cried out, — " Dive no more O sun!
Since thou must ever rise with hopeless hands;"
And, groaning, fell. Did we not marvel at
Her rising, as the widow at her son's?
Can Jane see this and live? — are you not listening?
   Col. I know not what you mean by all this firing,
Unless to empty barrels of old charges.
   Judge. Remove poor Willard in the shade.
   Col. What?
   Judge. (*Having misheard*).   Why?
The sunshine on his features is too dazzling
With ghastliness.
   Col. Sunshine!
   Judge.   Oh, any how
Move him from sight! behind there.
   Col. Not worth while.

Judge. Had we not better consult?
(*Both stare, each trying to read the other.*)
Col. About what?
Judge. What
We ought to do.
Col. Dispatch the wretch.
Judge. For what?
Col. Did he not lead us here designedly?
Judge. I said so ere I knew what I was saying,
Supported you impulsively — officially —
For firing like a murderer — lunatic —
Intending at first chance to reprimand you,
As Heli may have often done, poor fool!
No, by my hope in Christ no jot of guilt
Do I discern in him.
Col. Weak-sightedness
A witness? *Where*, pray? With this field-glass saw
I not the wretch pull back, as desperate oarsman
From vortex, long before poor Willard galloped
Upon the ledge?
Judge. What!
Col. Had I not, moreover,
Before that spied him bearing down on Willard?
Judge. Would Willard not have turned on him?
Col. He didn't.
Judge. Coward to not have sped to his assistance!
Col. I thought it was a feint.
Judge. It was a feint,
For Willard would have come back if in danger,
Not waded into the marsh still deeper.
Col. Deeper
He did go, hence is swallowed.
Judge. Oh! yet wait —
Col. Nay, saw him on his horse a standing serpent
In exultation as the General fell,
Then take to grassy groveling to slip off.
Judge. Judge him I will not; keep him under arrest.
(*Colonel starts.*) Where are you going?

Col. Shall be back soon.
Judge.   Counting
On my endorsement? Bear in mind, sir, never
Again shall I attach to a deed of rashness
My signature, — save to protest.
Col.   Hell! Will
People not think the general foully dealt with?
And this belief, like every other darkening
The earth, nay, all creation, must have victims.
You might as well pluck from a tiger's claws
A lambkin, as a thing belief is eating.
Judge. Lord! what would *you* do?
Col.   Let Belief eat on,
Nay, give her plenty of what she finds so toothsome.
Mobs in black masks, each howling like a demon
Against the Union, riddled us like woods
Between two batteries.
Judge. Riddled? Oh, how prove?
Col. I do not mind some flesh wounds.
Judge.   But I do.
No blood have I to spare, — and you?
Col.   Then riddle
Your hat, graze shoulder. Willard, dying, whispered
Within your ear —
Judge. When? when? did not —
Col.   Cannot
You say so?
Judge. Oh! —
Col.   That he had injured me
Through dread of being dubbed a nepotist, —
Judge. I, too, have suffered at his hands severely, —
Col. That, by suggestions, — worthy Jomini,
Whom Bonaparte feared, — I had opened the door
To the sky-ascending stairs, up which he led
Our country, like an invalid, or bride, —
Judge. But let it pass. The bush that we plant over
The dead should be well pruned, not have a thorn
Upon it to distress our fingers, wishes, —

Col. (*Showing impatience*). Though I am still a
  beggar under the steps,
Achingly perishing of cold neglect. —
Judge. But odoriferous flowers that may sustain
Us from the faint and fall —misanthropy. —
What now of that society?* Could it
Have throned him though?
Col. If it be large of limb,
I will make it our wrestler — Hiawatha, —
Against democracy, weak, brainless blusterer!
But tumble it, if small, and rise by standing
Upon its body. By destroying some one,
The public will declare us energetic. (*Starts.*)
Judge. Wait, such were well, if something better
  still, — (*catching Colonel*)
Are you stark mad? At such a sight will not
Poor Jane and country drop in epilepsy?
Col. (*Freeing himself.*) Damn it! no time to walk
  with an idea
Backward and forward, — cripples should be shot, —
Must spring on and spur off.
Judge. What! break our necks?
Col. Well!
Judge. Neither must behold such ghastliness.
  (*Col. Starts.*) Wait! wait! Am I a wolf that you
  should run?
    Would you not from your sister's mouth pluck
      poison?
Tell her I dare not, dare not; and dare you?
Col. How help it?

---

* "I design, in the following pages, to give some account of an extraordinary movement, set on foot of late by a few restless people, to establish imperialism in the United States. My intention is to show that there really exists a secret organization for this purpose, which has enrolled a considerable body of members; that the audacious print, called " *The Imperialist*," which appeared regularly every week during April, May, June, and July of the present year, was the accredited organ of the society; and that, though the paper has run its course, the society still continues." — L., *Galaxy for November, 1869.*

Judge. Know of only one thing.
Col. Well?
Judge. I hate it, shrink from it,
Col. Then let it drop.
Judge. Yet it will glove our numerous-fingered case
From numbing frost.
Col. Well?
Judge. Did you note their close
Resemblance?
Col. Whose?
Judge. Does he not look like Willard?
Col. What if he does?
Judge. Oh! do you think that he
Could — could —
Col. Could what?
Judge. Act Willard?
Col. What? ha! ha! (*Pushes him.*)
Judge. How dare you push me?
Col. Off to the mad-house!
Judge. What?
Col. There echo your heart and head out howling.
Judge. If
I err —
Col. If? ha! ha! ha!
Judge. Believe me, 'tis
From over sympathy, not lack of it.
Could I see Jennie bleeding as from lungs?
Col. Ha!
Judge. Could I see our country stricken down,
Nay, carried off by traitors, savages,
For mutilation?
Col. Bah! sheer gush!
Judge. Did not
Our party rescue her from degradation
Before?
Col. Yes.
Judge. Must he let her drop now?
Col. No.

Judge. Why not?
Col. Why not? We want to reap the pumpkins.
Judge. Tut, tut, sir! If he let her drop, would she
Not split her head wide open, so that death
Would crawl in like an hibernating bear?
Col. That is the way we put it when we stump.
Judge. Our country now depends for her existence
Upon one hair.
Col. One hair!
Judge. Aye, Willard's name.
Col. You mean our party.
Judge. Don't. Am I a dolt?
Know well what I am saying — mean our country.
Cut that one hair, she drops.
Col. If such a ghost,
She ought to drop. Why make a Frankenstein
Of her? I hate such bosh. More than a hair
Name needed, more than a blank, unloaded form.
Judge. The spirit is needed; — can't we be the spirit
As perfectly as Plover is the face?
Col. (*Slowly.*) That might go off.
Judge. Might? will.
Col. They did look twins;
Yet Jennie does sharp shooting with her eyes.
Judge. I think he could be chiseled to perfection,
Such things have been.
Col. We must do something.
Judge. Hurry,
He comes, — decide.
Col. (*After a pause.*) I honor the fourth commandment.
March on, I follow.
Judge. May the Lord —
Col. Here, here!
Put up no heavenly ensign, lest the devil
Take us for foes, turn grape and shell on us.
(*Fouracres and Plover enter.*)
Fouracres. He brags of a great conspiracy.

22   CAGLIOSTRO.

Judge. What, what, sir?
Fouracres. "In Denver alone," he says, "at present hundreds
Are at half-cock awaiting signals."
Plover.   Will
You guarantee my life if I drag up
Those getting away now?
Col. Drag each wretch up.
Plover.   Will
You take the names down?
Col. Yes.
Plover.   The rebel generals — but
They will themselves be here soon, and can answer.
Judge. We better defer all cross-examination
Until on safer ground.
Plover.   Just what I want,—
A trial, a public bath; just let me dive in,
Wash off cold, black suspicion from my skin.
Judge. Are you not guilty?
Plover. No.
Col.   Damn me if you
Get off so easily! confessed enough!
Plover. That I might get a trial.
Judge.   Were those credentials
Authentic?
Plover. Solid. Dead?
Col.   A blasted cap.—
Swear never to oppose our plan.
Judge. Swear, swear.
Plover. I swear to never oppose, but push it onward,—
Judge. Good!
Plover. Yere, wheelbarrow it from east to west
If needed, though I bend my shoulders over
Till, like a rainbow, they no more can straighten.
Judge. Oh! nothing on this earth is nobler, grander,
Than honest rainbow shoulders after the storm.
Col. Here, here.
Plover. Can I do more?

Col. Enough. (*To Judge.*) Untie him.
(*To Fouracres.*) Go to the tent, have it brought here.
[*Exit Fouracres.*]
Judge. (*Unshackling Plover.*) Ought bury
Him now?
Plover. Hey?
Col. Yes.
Plover. Be quick then, gents, for travelers
Aire not rare fish in this Gulf-stream of mountains, —
May any moment catch and gnaw the body.
Judge. Inter him quickly, I feel faint. — Look after
Effects.
Col. (*To Judge.*) You get the sword. He flung it off,
Seeing it added to his jeopardy,
He must have come down like a cataract
From crag to crag. There, see it glimmering.
Judge. Where?
Col. There,— hurry a bit ; I hate mere caterpillaring.
(*The Judge checking his impulse to retort, goes for the
 sword.*)
Don't tell the old man where we put the body.
Plover. If he should ask me, —
Col.   Misdirect him. — Swear
To never breathe of what you hear or see.
Fouracres. (*Entering with Pompey and Andrew carry-
ing the tent.*)
I swear.
Pompey and Andrew. I swar.
Col. Erect the tent there. (*To Plover.*) Lift.
(*Col. and Plover carry the body out through the groove.*)
Pompey. (*A dandy, and after a pause.*) What is de
 color of dis snake, dis trouble?
Andrew. Hush.
Pompey. Garter? rattle?
Andrew.   Swear we not to be
Deaf mutes?
Pompey. We can with muf one-sided yacht-like
Sail unobsarved, much better than by signs
Like de first fiddler. What has happened?

Fouracres. Hush.
Judge. (*After a pause, entering.*) Through yet?
Fouracres. Yes, Judge.
Plover. (*Entering.*) The Colonel wants you nigs.
[*Exeunt the three.*]
Judge. I now inaugurate you with his sword.
Plover. I had one once, but pawned it.
Judge. You have then
Had some experience?
Plover. I should think I had;
Was many a time a target company's captain.
(*Putting sword down.*) Lie down thar, snooze. If I
    must nurse you, rear you,
You will not keep so rosy-cheeked, I reckon,
But wane a skeleton.
Judge. Oh! rosy-cheeked
With running up the hill of victory
With Fatherland and Freedom by the hand,
Parents whose faces may well beam with pride.
Col. (*Entering.*) Who else was thought of for the
    emperorship?
Plover. The biggest-handed.
Col. Named?
Plover. No.
Judge. Who?
Plover. Whoever
Can hold the reins of all the states at once
Without permitting a horse to balk or stop,
Or over-jump his traces, and can drive
Where snow is thick, so as to give the people
A jolly time, a picnic, not a dump.
Could you, sir?
Col. Easily.
Judge. (*Muttering.*) Like Phaeton.
Plover. When I broached it, the General, with a look
Which wound around me like a whip, *spurred off.*
Who?
Judge. You yourself may have to drive.

Col. How?
Plover. Me?
I could not drive a district, drive a sulky,
Without a rough-and-tumble, smash-up.
Judge. That
Is, — as a child in some big person's lap.
Plover. I see, I drive when your hands get too cold,
Or when the coast is clear, has no more turns.
Judge. Exactly.
Col. Drop this project.
Judge. Why, sir?
Plover. Caché it?
Col. Yes; do not dig it up till you get orders.
Plover. All right, boss.
Col. You can take your rig right off.
Plover. (*Scratching his ear.*) Before I get another to put on?
Col. No, they lag long;
Judge. Sworn in?
Col. Yes.
Judge. Whither sent?
Col. To dig a rifle pit out — mean a grave.
Judge. Why is it that he has to change his clothes?
Col. Damn it, am I before court martial, or
Committee on the conduct of the war?
Judge. You need not snap so. Do you think interment
Quite safe? Cremation would be safer.
Col. Need
A good retrenchment to ward off disaster
If we are worsted, cannot further advance.
Judge. If it were taken by the enemy, —
Col. Ere that we burn it, as the Russians, Moscow.
Judge. When, when incinerate it?
Col. Not before
The marriage.
Judge. Oh! the marriage! how? how?
Col. How
Do I know? you proposed it; should have known
The enemy's strength before attacking him.

Judge. I did not dare to think of that before.
I pushed it off with the thought that we were leaving
Poor Willard like a dog upon the ground.
    Col. Would he not be locked up in a room, if home?
    Judge. Would be laid out in state. Neglect, atrocious!
    Col. During the battle can we kneel and whimper
Over a fallen brother? Onward! onward!
Must trample the dearest down,— shell even the churches
If in the way.
    Judge. Hey!
    Col. Onward! fire! Is the rite
Essential?
    Judge. Are we brutes?
    Col.   Unluckily, no.*
How get a minister? or Jane's consent?
    Judge. Until the marriage not another step.
    Col. I differ in opinion.
    Judge.   Oh! would crash
Poor Jennie's eyes and head in with this horror
Ten thousand times, rather than she should live
Unholily like — Oh! Oh! Oh!
    Plover. (*To Col.*)   Does spanking
Cross youngsters make them quiet? never. Hope
Should take his feelings in her arms, walk up
And down the floor, sing hushabye.
    Col.   What hope?
See none.
    Plover. Believe in spirits?
    Col. Trash!
    Plover.   Was thinking
Of Squigginson.
    Col. The juggler?
    Plover.   Medium,— Sampson —
Long white-haired — down back — drest all yaller?
    Col. Why?
    Plover. Bet he could get us spirits to pump out

---

* Edward von Hartmann.

This vessel, which is now so full of water
We splash at every step.
  Judge. But could he, though?
  Plover. Well, if he can't, no man now kicking can.
Lincoln and cabinet once consulted him.
  Judge. True! I was present.
  Col.   Trash!
  Judge. What's trash, sir?
  Col. Spirits.   [*Exit.*]
  Plover. I laughed at them, jeered, sneered, until my
    nose
Was plucked by one — Oh! twisted with a corkscrew —
Or with a dentist's or a blacksmith's pinchers. (*Feels his
    nose.*)
I fancy it a ram's horn ever since.
  Judge. Could there have been no trick?
  Plover.   A trick of course,
But then it was a ghost who played it.
  Col. (*Re-entering.*)   Strip,—
Fouracres comes with regimentals.
  Plover. (*To Fouracres, entering in a heat.*) What's
The matter?
  Judge. Chased?
  Fouracres.   I ran because the Colonel
Said I should hurry up, and clouds were gathering.
  Judge. Oh!
  Plover. Have I not seen you at Squigginson's?
  Fouracres. Have been at circles.
  Plover. Have seen spirits?
  Fouracres. Yes, sir.
  Plover. Did any fish up sea-sunk secrets?
  Judge. Hey?
  Col. That you had eaten garlic for your dinner?
  Fouracres. Said I was hankering after Miss Matilda,
That I had married a thief disguised as woman
Which made me swear to never risk another,
For that pug nose had been my family's wet nurse.*

* Dr. Draper. Milk.

That my dear sister Kate had, when nineteen,
Though 'till then white as milk, become a negress,
The blackest, woolliest,—*
   Judge. True?
   Fouracres. True as I live,—
And that she took to it quite handsomely,
For, in three weeks, she married a colored preacher.
   Col. Had she known him before?
   Fouracres. From creeping-hood.
   Col. Ha! clearly a case of mind controlling matter.
They loved each other ardently,—
   Fouracres. No, Colonel.
   Col. Had seen Othello, read it to each other.
   Fouracres. No, Colonel; no! no!
   Judge. (*To Fouracres.*) To the medium, sir.
   Col. The preacher would have whitened — which so
     few do —
If he had been the stronger in his mind.
   Judge. Fly to the medium, fetch him quickly hither.
In all my life I never met a witness
So tantalizing with irrelevancy.
   Col. Ere I consent, sir, promise to support
My plan when yours has failed.
   Judge. Wait till it does fail.   [*Exit Fouracres.*]
   Col. This medium may be able to entrance
Dear Jennie, but will he not play the devil
With her poor mind? (*To Fouracres.*) *Put lightning to
   your heels.*
(*To Plover.*) Change clothing quickly.
   Plover. Now, I don't deny
That we may have to hang in dark suspense
In seances sometime, like hams and shoulders
Within a smoke house.
   Col. Damn it. (*To Fouracres.*) Hey! hey! hey!
(*To Plover.*) Should said so first.
   Judge. (*To Fouracres.*) Go on!

      * Complexion. *Appleton's Encyclopedia.*

Plover. But will be cured.
Andrew. (*Re-entering.*) De garments.
Col.   Follow! under no pretense
Whatever must he slip your grip of sight.
Remember promises.
                    [*Exit nervously with Andrew.*]
Plover. Pull off that boot, Judge.
  (*The Judge, after hesitating a few seconds, complies*)
And must I change my good old honest name?
It is a porous plaster covering me
From head to foot, and pulling off hurts, hurts.
Gosh! 'tis like leaving home with mother standing
At door, or gate, white-aproning her red eyes,
And sister at the fence, with yellow head
Down, like the willow over the old man's grave.
  Judge. Hurry! — what standing for?
  Plover.   Some tears of memory
Just gathered in my eyes, but now are shed.
I hate to shake this rig.
  Col. (*Entering*).   You must have hated
To shake it for some months.
  Plover.   Gosh! just what Sal
Was in the habit of ejaculating;
For dust, least straw, will set a woman cracked,
As a red shirt will set a bullock crazy.
  Col. Is she still living?
  Plover.   Yere, and ruther tough;
Last week's collision barely skinned her nose.
  Judge. And are you married?
  Plover. Many a wretched year.
  Judge. Mountains on mountains rise, — how cross
        them all?
  Col. One at a time.
  Plover.   What aire you going to do
With these old things?
  Col.   Put them upon the body
That clues may point to your demise, not his,
Should any harass us on flank, or rear.

Judge. Clues!
Col. (*To Plover.*) Get in there. (*Plover enters tent.*)
Judge. Where is the grave?
Col. No matter To you.
Judge. But 'tis.
Col. 'Tis not.
Judge. Must read the service.
Col. If he be now in Heaven, can you improve him?
No other place to go to.
Judge. Isn't there though?
'Twere well for you there were not.
Col. You, fire-proof?
Combustible as I am.
Judge. Oh! more so,
A thousand times more so! more so indeed!
I am neck deep, but not yet overhead;
One gasp more, not too late yet to be saved.
Col. Hell! (*Starts off.*)
Judge. (*Wringing his hands and turning aside.*)
Oh! that gnashing famine after God,
That famine fever for one drop of peace.
(*Glancing at Colonel and following.*)
George! George! Come back! I say, *come back! come back!*

ACT II.

(PLOVER *in regimentals under the awning.*)

Judge. (*Approaching.*) I called you, why did you not come and stop him?
Plover. I had no shooter, and the Colonel's quick,—
And, Judge, I took the pledge from interfering
In family squabbles just three years last Fourth,
When, rushing to the rescue of a woman

Screaming "help! murder!" she was first to turn
Upon me with a poker, crying, " Fritz,
Now make yourselfs vonce handy mit stove-covers
Against dis tief, or mit your razor vitch
You jus vos daking out to cut mine corns."
Bloods thicker than water, — it will heal its cut
Quicker than cobwebs, or black plaster, Judge.
(*Judge scowls.*) Cramps? got 'em bad, Judge?
   Judge. No, no.
   Plover.   Thought you had.
(*Rubbing his knees.*)   A storm comes, I can feel it in my
    bones.
   Judge. Fouracres yet in sight? my eyes are dusking.
   Plover. Not yet.
   Judge. Suppose the doctor be from home, —
   Plover. What good is such supposing? I have heard
The best preventive of a bloody nose
Is just to keep it clean of ugly places.
Why stick our noses into mere supposing,
Then have them bleeding, make success, on coming
Up, puffing, drop his cold keys down our back
Instead of opening the doors at once.
   Col. (*Entering.*)   Fouracres not yet back?
   Plover.   Not yet.
   Judge.   The grave
Is all right I suppose, —
   Col. Suppose it is.
   Judge. No danger — not the slightest — of discovery?
   Col. No more than of your ever hushing up.
Ask me at once, sir, if I am stark mad.
   Judge. I need not ask about a thing I see.
   Col. We start right off without that charlatan.
Oh, idiot that I was to have consented
One second! There is something, not ourselves,
That makes for evil, as for righteousness.
   Judge. (*Warmly*) We Christians call that Satan.

Col. We!
Judge. Oh!
Col. (*To Plover.*) Sicken.
Plover. Sicken?
Col. Assume a disease that alters features,
As Walter Raleigh did to save his life.
Plover. He did, hey? How wind up?
Col. How ignorant!
Judge. How manage the marriage?
Col. During his convalescence
We can treat that, as well as how to lessen
Ourselves of clumsy luggage. Have we not
His project to dispose of, and his spouse?
Plover. Gosh! I forgot poor Sal — as usual.
Judge. Was
She ever unfaithful?
Plover. No.
Judge. Too bad! bad case!
I would advise desertion for two years.
Plover. Only two years?
Col. Damn it, man, are you raving?
Plover. Expected next his hand out for the fee.
Judge. Were she unfaithful, we could feel less culpable.
(*Pacing.*) Oh! swarms of thoughts are beetling in my
    face,
They bite and blind so, that I feel half mad.
The marriage when arranged, how end?
Plover. With
A twenty pounder through the future's broad side,
Smoke-stack, or rigging.
Judge. (*In anguish.*) Oh!
Plover. All clouds above us
Will snow in our favor fast and thick the moment
The medium comes. A reindeer I shall be
With bells to the nuptial sled. Gosh! I can see
Myself a flying and the country taking
A hitch behind.

Judge. The snow may turn to rain,
Make swamping slush. Why was I ever born?
 Col. I give it up, if not to be a plague.
 Judge. Back!
 Col. Never.
 Judge. Where is Andrew? where Fouracres?
They took our finest horses, —
 Col. As I ordered
Them.
 Judge. Ha! the more the idiot, fool!
May be they start the human cry against us.
 Plover. This secret is indeed too small a boat
For more than three to sit in.
 Col. We must tumble
The others over, else go down to bottom.
 Judge. Murder? murd —
 Col. Damn you, hush.
 Judge. Damn! damn! Oh! Oh!
 Plover. Can we keep up a steady pull from sight,
If we are wedged in — have not elbow room —
And have to carry three huge lifeless bulks?
No one but pullers can remain aboard,
Except the cockswain. (*To Judge.*) You must be the
  cockswain,
Though must not blur your eyes with tears, then fancy
Thick fog ahead.
 Judge. Were it not better, sir,
To catch those runaways than, unpetitioned,.
To give instructions?
 Plover. Judge, you hit bull's eye.
 Judge. Fouracres seemed in hissing howling woods,
Striving to keep in shriek till out of them.
 Col. Had he so seemed, you would have tightened
  grip.
 Plover. What can he do? can't three outswear a
  moke?
 Col. No negro. (*Goes to the side*)
 Judge. (*Following him.*) Are they coming?

Plover.   I'll be hanged
If he ain't turning like his milky sister
Love lightninged then.   He has some "yock! yock!
    yah!"
With arms akimbo on the brain.   When thousands
Of lovers lose themselves in smallest mouths,
As skylarks in the rosy mouth of morn,—
Which may be why to kiss is called skylarking,—
No wonder he is lost in one so roomy.
     Judge. Land! land!   The doctor, too?
     Col.   No, nor Fouracres.
     Judge. Lord!
     Col. You have fired and missed, it is my turn.
     Judge. Oh! Lord! wait,— not my signature — no, no.
     Col. When the barometer drops down so fast,
And ship is listing so that none can stand,
Must we not make like lightning to the shore?
     Plover. (*To Judge.*)   May be the land the Colonel
    spies is nearer;
The blue upon its hills may be a jay
Let loose from the ark of spring.
     Col. (*To Andrew rushing in.*)   Where is Fouracres?
     Judge. What can have happened? where is he?
    where? where?
Oh! where?
     Andrew. De table swallowed him.
     Judge. What!
     Col.   Idiot,
Did I not tell you under no pretence
To let him slip your grip of sight?
     Andrew.   Yes, Colonel,
But I was hauled up by de heels, like bulls
In slaughter-houses, pelted out de winder.
     Col. A put up job! By the Eternal, I
Will scatter some one's brains like melon seed.
Fouracres and that juggler are in league.
     Judge. Then jump upon them ere they creep away
Swiftly as swallows.

Plover. Have seen marvels beating
All hollow those the moke has just related.
These are the first plucks that the doctor gives
His goose-like banjo, ere he plays his best.
   Judge. What did the doctor say?
   Andrew.   He was not home, sar.
   Judge. Oh! knew that once we cut adrift from God,
He would not send an angel to our rescue,
But let us dash a-down the dark canon.
   Col. (*To Andrew.*) Where is Fouracres's horse?
   Andrew. Sar? at de doctor's.
   Col. Go after that rascal; show not up without him.
   Judge. Come back of *course*, if you can't find him.
   Col.   Hush!
   Judge. Because one goes, lose all?
   Col. (*Writing.*)   This to your lady.
   Judge. I look up and I see no sky, no hope,
But sand-storms bursting down and walls collapsing.
   Plover. You need not fret, the doctor will be here.
                                        (*Lightning twice.*)
   Judge. Oh!
   Plover. Bright-winged swallows speeding, like por-
      poises.
Ahead of the storm, above white cranking ganders,
Drawing green chains of goslings from the pond.
Gosh! I can see them Indian file, hear mother,
With switch behind her, shouting, "Don't dare roll
Down them wet trowsers, but just fall in line." (*Rubs
    his legs.*)
   Judge. As we to death. Oh! had you hindered this,
                            [*Exit Andrew with note.*]
Which by one word, one beck, you still can do, —
As, when a child, I would have hindered you
From hanging, drowning, — but you drive me on.
   Col. Mere arguing now is vain, our ship is burning.
   Judge. But we can quench the blaze.
   Col. Too late.   (*Thunder.*)
   Judge. No, no!

Col. Ah! in my soul, sir, you have generated
A huge ambition, and he now is howling
For something to eat and wear. Far too athletic
Is he — tall, strong — for me to throw, or choke,
Were I inclined to a deed so parricidal — (*Thunder.*)
"Would you not from your sister's mouth pluck poi-
    son!" [*Col. coughs and goes out for air.*]
  Judge. Ah me! Oh, misery, misery! I am damned.
(*Clutching Plover.*) You join us willingly?
  Plover. Most willingly.
  Judge. You will not at your death cry out to Heaven
To blast to hell this wretch, white sepulchre, —
This head that has Saint Elmo's light of age
Upon it, ship see-sawing on the verge
Between two gulches of the sea, or earthquakes,
A horrible black past, still blacker future?
  Col. (*Returning.*) Hell!
  Judge. Endless gnashing famine after God! — (*To
Plover.*) This white hair that should be the dawning
    rays
Of a felicitous eternity, —
Humanity's Pike's Peak at *Sun-rise*, —
  Plover. (*Trying to release himself gently, while the
    Colonel plucks the Judge.*) No! —
  Judge. Not glare of death, the comet that strikes earth
Each day, nay, hour, and shakes vast millions off.
  Col. Let go.
  Judge. Swear! swear!
  Plover. I swear.
  Judge. (*Releasing Plover.*) I did my best.
To catch up and protest. (*Paces rapidly then stops.*) I
    ran as far
As I was able, shouting, "Stop! come back!" —
  Plover. (*To Col.*) The rumbling ere the mental quake,
    I reckon.
  Judge. Can more have been expected? Stupid fool!
I should have known swift horses always stand
In readiness for Evil to spring on, —

Plover. (*To Col.*) Ought we not keep at door, valise
  in hand?
Judge. That in a thrice he is beyond our grasp
To pierce us flying, — diabolic Parthian !
     (*On the rocks to the right rises a blue cloud.*)
  Col. Now ready for the road ?
  Judge. Lord! in this storm?
  Col. The clouds are but a black horse cavalry
And will be off on making a dash or two.
  Judge. Ah! but just such —
  Col. I know, I know.
  Judge.   What do
You know? but little, and that nonsense. Had
You taken my advice, sir, which you never
Did — (*pauses.*)
  Col. Say it out ! that I was carried off
By such a dash, then left among the dead, —
No more than able to crawl across a few days, —
Red, ghastly, mangled bodies pestering earth.
Shake me no more up, whispering, "look! look! look!"
Afraid that I will nap from agony
One minute? What the devil am I doing
But following your advice most docily ?
  Judge.   Ha !
No rational child will burn his fingers twice
At the same fire.
  Col. (*Donning a rubber coat and hat.*) Fetch him at
  once to the house.
The darky will have swept the ice from path,
And I will call on Squigginson. Fouracres
Will meet us with the carriage on the road.
  Judge. I hope so.
  Col. Damn your hope so!
  Plover.   Scissors, Colonel ?
Willard looked like my double candle lighted
Upon the wall, or ruther I looked his. (*Lightning.*)
  Judge. (*Pulling George back.*) No scissors during the
  lightning! no! no! no!

Col. (*Turning.*) Pshaw! That infernal storm will
  keep her back.
Judge. From where?
Col. The school where she is to await us.
Judge. During her absence are we to effect
An entrance? Oh, house-breakers, verily!
Come, come; not innocent now, as when you clomb
The poplar, high above the red-bird's nest,
To see whence lightning came.
  Col. Fain would I climb
To see how far this lightning is to go.
  Judge. To fathomless perdition, with us after
It, like poor whalers tangled in their rope. (*Lightning.*)
Come!
  Col. Hide behind the palm-leaf if you will,
I smother, — must have air.
  Judge. (*To Plover.*) Close up without him!
(*Thunder, the tent is closed and the Col. after pausing,
  descends the slope speedily.*)
  Cagliostro. (*Evolving from the blue cloud, and great
    thunder and lightning.*)
Thou white fool, comest thou to harass me?
Art thou, wierd white of arm of the cloud, now shaken
At earth to scare her from my mirages?
Men who are billowed into consternation
And high resolving under thy wan waving,
Are rippleless when thou art withered up. (*Thunder.*)
  Dr. Squigginson. (*Entering,*)
These are the rocks to which the telegram *
Directed me, which nature sculptured dozing,
And which religion and society
Have taken for their models in constructing
Their presses, as if hearts and souls were cheese.
O, light of the world, Arabula! hail! hail!
  Cag. No more the saddest sight to man, or God,
The burning of a mind down into ashes,

---

* Andrew Jackson Davis. "*The Diakka and their Earthly Victims.*"

Like lone log building in canon, on boulder,
Or on the rock in middle of the lake,
Where, dizzy with beauty, wild birds whirl about;
No, nor will poverty transform a man
A scorpion, hating, hated, stinging, stung.
No more will age, the white owl, pounce on men,
Drag them like worm-heaps to his haunt, the tomb;
Nor will distempers, which now lurk in swamps,
Seize cities, tear them with their teeth and talons,
Dash off with them down brinks to desolation,
The lake, thus in their own age making them
Lake dwellings.
 Dr. Glorious!
 Cag.   This Messiah will flood
All earth, drear stenching mud, with joy, blue sea
Drawn off by un-Promethean false religion,
Black hugest water-spout, then upward drifted
Till frozen into long white streaks of clouds,
Cold perches for the weary-winged vision
Of mortals.
 Dr.   Is the woman, armed with babe,
Who was to have revolved the crank before,
To come now?
 Cag. No.
 Dr.   Who?
 Cag.   Lilla Lamb.
 Dr.   Who?
 Cag.   Lilla.
 Dr. When I left Lilla, her death-frosted eyes
Were fastened on the wall, like lifeless flies.
You mock me, toss me over on my back,
As boys kick tortoises.
 Cag.   When clouds, red, orange,
And white, whirl up the east, as in the desert
Pillars of sand, you gladden, knowing that
The sun, the fire tornado, is approaching;
On meeting Lilla, you will wax hilarious,
As the red-cock, by flapping thousands echoed,

For you will find her clouded gorgeously,
Will feel the heat of the luminous hurricane,
Which is to set your error-crushing mill
In ceaseless-wheeling motion.
  Dr.   Gracious spirit,
How? how?
  Cag.   How is the reign of the upper powers
Who will not drop it, cognizant that man
With it would be an earth-destroying Phaeton;
Enough for him to have the glorious ride.
  Dr. Without the how, will mind continue not
To dash upon the rocks of pain, despair,
Be billows plunging down with arm-hid faces?
  Cag. No. Mind will rest, as goat on a sunny jag.
The Savior will be born before cock-crow
To-night at Willard's house.
  Dr. When? where? Oh!
  Cag. (Disappearing.)   Lilla
May not be needed there, and yet she may;
If strong of mind, she can project her spirit
Thither, as angler his long leaded line.
Go to the tent where you are in request.
  Dr. Benignant spirit! Save I read souls, minds,
As well as kidneys, lungs, nay, rightly mate them,
Which is the main thing, — not the hawk with herring,
The snake with eel, nor weed with flower, nor boar
With gay gazelle, nor tiger with milch cow,
Eagle with goose, nor camel with humped cat,
That one may choke, outrun, eat, rend, the other,
Or race companionless with sun from clearance
In cloud to clearance, wooded stream to stream, —
I see no hope for man. Illumine not
The labyrinth of life, if thou thereby
Increase its shadows; if thy stream from heaven
Channel no outing for humanity.
(*East and west the rain dashes and the sun bursts
    grandly, at which sight the doctor is transfixed
    with delight; but he soon descends evincing by his*

stops and gestures great perturbation. As the Colonel enters, Patsy, white-sheeted and eating a pumpkin, appears.) *

Patsy. With pumpkin one hits two birds at one welt,
Two vultures, clawing hunger and thirst!
    (*Opens the tent and whispers in the Judge's ear.*)
Judge. (*Coming out followed by Plover.*) A spirit
Could that have been?
    Col.   Maybe it was not closed,
Or one of us did it unconsciously.
    Judge. You lie, sir, and you know it. (*To Plover.*)
        Did you hear
A voice?
    Plover. No.
    Judge.   Not that I must offer up
My darling, even as Abraham did Isaac,
Or Jephthah, robed in victory warm, his daughter?
For God is thirsting for a cold, clear drink
Out of the hard, green-crusted pool of earth.
    Col. Why listen to the buzzing of delusions?
Catch them and crush them ere they bite your brain,
Causing your hands, when full of work, to open
And let all drop that they may rub, rub, rub.
    Judge. Delusion! Are you not my son? I wish
That were a delusion.
    Col.   So do I.
    Judge.   How snappish,
You cur!
    Col. (*To Plover.*) Now ready?
    Plover.   Going to trim my beard?
        (*Col. darts for the scissors savagely.*)
Must I face her to-night?
    Col.   Yes.

---

* A spirit told Professor Phelps that he was in hell, and liked pumpkin pie. — *Charles Beecher.*

Plover.   Why not put
The meeting off till I am better prepared, —
A week, a month?
   Col.   To-morrow Willard's father
Will come and make poor Jane most miserable,
For he denies her Emma has been found.
   Judge. We cannot tempt his David's sling of sight
Till armored far completer than Goliath,
And now we are as nude as savages.
               (*Patsy re-appears eating pumpkin.*)
   Plover. The first shot of her eyes may blow my head
off.
   (*Sits but jumps up when the Colonel's elbow is pulled
         by Patsy.*)
I'll play off — oh! — for heaven's sake grease that saw,
Else lay me bodily upon a buck.   (*Sits.*)
   Col. Sit quiet. (*Trims somewhat, even after being
again pulled.*)
   Plover.   Hold on! hey! hello there! ho!
(*Jumping.*)   Those aire no scissors, but a rasp, or rat-
      trap.
Each puck was like an eye-tooth being drawn,
Or rosy smeller twisted from the stem, —
Sharpen those blunts, or give chloroform.   (*Sits.*)
   Judge. Just let me do the cutting.
   Col.   Hold his head.
         (*Judge holds it and the Colonel cuts.*)
   Plover. Ho! ho!
   Col.   Keep still.
   Plover.   Hello!
   Col. (*To Judge.*)   Hold tighter.
   Plover.   (*Jumping up.*)   Ho!
I am no goose, plum-pudding, public treasury,
To stand such plucking.
   Judge.   This, a time for pleasantry?
Laughing? — at us?
   Col.   Sit.
   Plover. (*Sitting to Judge.*)   No.

Judge. (*Stepping aside.*) How mocking laughter
Will open wide its morning-glory mouths
Over our grave yet! Oh, to have to pull
His boot off — in all senses! —
    Plover   Ho! gee ho!
Ho!
    Col. That will do.
    Plover.   Thank heaven. Here comes the doctor.
                              (*Goes to meet him.*)
    Judge. (*Pulling Col. aside.*)
Close to the grave have you a sign, a light,
Which neither blast nor torrent can extinguish?
    Col. (*Dashing away.*)
Am I a gawk to quit a place, expecting
My shadow to remain a sentinel?
    Plover. (*With doctor.*) The Colonel, Judge. (*They salute each other.*)
    Col. Where is Fouracres?
    Dr.   Who
Is he?
    Col. My servant.
    Dr. (*Piqued by the Colonel's rudeness.*) In or out of flesh,
Within my sight or invocation, sir.
    Col. (*Muttering.*) Tight in his grasp.
    Dr. Why am I wanted here?
    Plover. I'm horrid sick.
    Dr. You? Strange! I see your works, —
You being to me a watch with case flung open, —
Heart, liver, kidneys, lungs, — see no disorder.
    Col. He and his wife fell out, —
    Judge.   For a mere nothing.
    Plover. Says I, Sall, Templeton is out here sporting
For pocket, Heaven that he can never cram enough.
On no account let that good man, —
    Col.   Here, here.
    Plover. For you remember the talk that once was loud,

Within a forty foot pole of your ear,
It being blackest ice within that distance.
"Confounded liar!" says she.
 Judge.   Oh!
 Plover.   Words grow up
To blows, as girls with tempers softly furred
To women with long claws, you know.
 Judge.   She was
In the right.
 Plover. She was, hey?
 Col.   Women always are.
 Judge. (*To Dr.*) His first wife was an earthquake, and he trembles
Yet from the shock that laid his home in ruins.
 Col. To make a long tale short, he must be sick,
For she will then capitulate.
 Dr. (*Indignantly starting.*) Good day.
 Judge. Wait!
 Col. What is up?
 Dr.   What you desire is a quack,
Some rich practitioner long habituated
To treating ladies, who forget, nor seldom,
The taste of health, champagne, ambrosia, till
They sip disease, face-souring vinegar. (*Staggers.*)
 Col. Do we expect your services for nothing?
 Judge. See!
(*Dr. falls into a chair and vices his head between his knees.*]
 Plover. Set him off by asking what you want.
 Judge. I know not what to ask. (*The Judge falls, the chair that he flings himself into being pulled by Patsy. The Colonel turns aside that he may not be a witness.*
 Patsy. (*Whispering to Dr.*) Me hoop-skirt tripped [*]
His chair up: faix, I'm sorry, and beg pardon.

---

[*] Once, when Mr. Davenport senior was sitting, tilted back on the hind legs of his chair, he was suddenly thrown over backward. Afterwards a spirit apologized for the accident, "the hoops of her crinoline having caught under the raised leg of the chair in passing."— *T. L. Nichols, M. D.*

(*Lifts a chair and sings*)
O, were ye the emperor, traitor, who
First blackens Washington's sate, — O !
A plucked Thanksgiving's goose would you
Be, held up thus by the fate, — O !
  Judge. Did you hear that ?
  Col. Heard nothing, nor did you.
(*Patsy places the chair on the Colonel's head, pulls his
  nose, and jumps up and down twice in front of him.
  The Colonel dashes the chair off, seems dizzy, and
  mutters, rubbing his eyes.*)   The opium is at work.
  Plover.   What ails me, doctor?
  Dr. Hither I see the General galloping,
The peaks before him like a camp of tents.
He trips, —
  Judge.   God !
  Dr.   Falls.
  Col.   Betrayed !
  Plover.   You trot too fast
Across the shaky bridge, the sign says "Walk."
  Dr. Look! into him a vulgar spirit dashes,
As suddenly as rain from cloudless sky,
Or buccaneers, — to whose light craft, mere saddle,
The wave with camel back is camel-footed, —
Board vessels laden low and oxen-tugged.
Behold the conflict! Willard's spirit, like
A ship on billow, falls to mount aloft,
The only wise a brave soul ever falls,
And, as he enters Mars, all stand, each shouting
With an Achillian voice, " Hail to the Chief ! '
Now blinding brilliancy, the curtain of God,
Excludes me from the banquet, and, with hunger
For shade, I seek the earth ; but blazing horror
Scorches my eyes. A man, white-haired, world-honored,
With face averted from his daughter, drags
Her to the stake, all bleeding — lacerated —
  Judge. God !
  Dr. From her hair, disheveled like the plumage

Of hen when sheltering brood from hovering hawk,
Down to her slender waist, along arms, breast.

Judge. My darling, run! Deny me! — were I dead —
Col. Hush!

Dr. What a carmine-mouthed and pawed black growler
Close at her heels!

Judge. I am that bloody dog.

Dr. Behold! would he be Abraham? He lifts
The trembling blade, but it is dashed a clinker
Into the ground, by a ball of lightning.

Judge. (Relieved.) Oh!

Col. (Tossing the Dr.'s chair over and seizing him.)
No time for this damned humbug, I must have
My servant.

Judge. Let him go, George! let him go.

Col. (To Dr.) Where that deserter — from insane.
asylum —
Whom we decoy back, through philanthropy,
He having been in our service many years?

Judge. All that you say is true — true to the letter,—
But, —

Col. But be damned. *(To Dr.)* I want him; do you
hear?

Dr. (Struggling.) Force is no key for any door of mine,
You ruffian! brute!

Plover. (Pulling Colonel who jerks away.) You better let him go.

Dr. Unhand me, instantly, or my familiar, —
Not spongy-fingered, I admonish you,—
Will teach you something you will never forget.

Col. Take me for a damned idiot, or a woman?

Dr. Spirit, convince him — *gently!*

Judge. (Whiningly.) A big idiot
Indeed! Was not the chair upon your head,
The elbow plucking, and my fall enough?

Col. (Releasing Dr. and turning on Judge.) Drunk!
crazy! trash! *(Patsy blows a fish-horn at the Colonel's ear, and around his neck puts a string of bull-frogs.)*

Judge. Oh!
Col. You damned juggler! making
Of me a target? (*Rushes at Dr. but stops, having flour dashed into his face by Patsy, who then wipes it off with a blacking brush.*] *
Judge. Blinded like Saint Paul
By lightning.
Plover. Flour, Judge. — Colonel, give it up,
You cannot hold the cramping battery out.
(*Patsy flings torpedoes at the Colonel's feet.*)
Col. Hell and damnation! If all Presidents, † —
(*Pinched on shoulders and legs alternatively by Patsy who rises to a great height, drops, and sometimes plays dog, the Colonel's rubbing and snatching with both hands on all sides, become desperate, his language more and more emphatic. Plover and the Judge, in whose faces Patsy occasionally fillips beans, step about lively, and the Doctor, folding his arms, smiles.*)
All Senators, — all Representatives, —
Chief Justices with their associates, —
Dr. He goes a crabbing with two bursted nets.
Col. Nay, all mankind, — including even myself, —
Should swear they saw a spirit pluck my elbow,
Or heard one whisper, " offer up thy daughter," —
Ridiculous!
Dr. Or put you through the mill,
Or thought your head was leather, dirty shoe,
Or diamond-necklaced you with croaking bull-frogs, —
Col. Or aught unnatural prated of by fools —
As that a man and woman cannot light their taper
Of love, to go down crooked, steep, dark life,
But at an altar, —
Judge. Ha! no! no! her head
Split open were a sunrise of delight —
To which I would cry, rise no more, no more,
Since you must ever rise with hopeless hands, —

* Judge Edmonds. † James Parton, " *Topics of the Times.*"

Col. Would I be so fat-witted a renegade —
Judge. (*Grasping at his escaped thought.*)
That I may ever bask in your bright breathing
Upon the world, like Christ on his apostles. —
    Col. From science — asinine — as ever to let
Such follies with their muddy sandals enter
The Holy of Holies, my belief? (*Starts, but his leg, in
    the act of kicking, is caught and lifted by Patsy,
    who afterwards puts an immense pumpkin on his
    head. After a minute's effort the Colonel works
    it off.*)
Judge.   Fool! idiot!
Dr. (*To Col.*) Require more proofs of immortality?
Judge. The fool, depreciating, shakes his head
So violently that he shakes it off —
Off — off — if it were ever — ever on.
    Dr. He thinks Voltaire, Paine, Strauss, view him, —
        cry " bravo!"
    (*Steps aside, gazes about, and then addresses Col.*)
Not one of them is here now, I assure you.
    Judge. No, never has joy alighted on my heart
But when exhausted, white eyed, broken winged,
Dark with the shadow of the grasping hawk,
(*To Col.*) Which you have always been. It made me
    happy
To think Jane might not be precipitated,
But might ride on.
    Col. (*Flung down.*) Oh!
    Judge.   George! George!
    Col.   Hush.
    Plover.   Hurt, Colonel?
    Patsy. So falls the country, age, that kicks at hiven.
How can ye proshper, kicking at your bethers?
    Judge. It is not raining now.
        (*Walks then tumbles out.*)
    Dr.   Why his contortions?
    Patsy. Bedad I thinks he has the prickly hate,
Or like the pracher that George Francis Train

Was fond of spaking of, he must have left
His breeches and his shirt out for to droy,
Not draming that a drunken set of hornets
Would stagger into thim, and niver waken
Till he was in the pulpit emphasizing
Some whopper with a clap upon his knay.
(*Mimics the Colonel, and, catching Plover slipping out,
leads him back by the nose.*)
Ye are the corduroys I must step into.
   Dr. Did you hear that?
   Col.   Heard nothing, nor did you.
Produce my servant instantly, or,—
   Dr. (*Coolly, and pointing at Plover tumbled by Patsy,
who disappears.*)   Well,
Sir, that not most delectable?
   Plover.   Gee! Ho!
I pity the whale that swallowed Jonah — Oh!
   Col. Out-generaled! no, no, damn me if I will be.
(*Catches Plover who pinches him.*)
I will not have this hazing here; nor pinching;
You did the pinching before, perfidious villain!
   Plover. Oh! (*Gyrates his arms, and seeing pen, ink,
and paper, writes.*)
   Dr. (*Pulling Colonel.*) To philosophers, thumps,
pinches, tumblings,
Are not essentials, minus which minds god-like
Groan, gnawed with hunger, but mere accidents,
Burs worth considering for the meat they cover.
Be manly, flee from sophistry, nor wait
Till, rat-like, smoked out with excessive light.
   Col. Your orders,— (*muttering*) I must have that
black —
   Dr.   Shall hold
A seance at the General's house at ten.—
See!
   Col. (*Snatching paper.*) Hell! on the copy of my dis-
quisition
On frogs.

Dr.　　No matter,—a message for mankind!—
Though on the black waste, too, where were the harm?
Whatever truth has been by ancient thinkers
Vellumed or spoken, or by young ones penned,
Is found in my revelations, freed from dross.*
Did Judas have red beard? or spill the salt?
No, it was sandy; what he spilt was pepper.
What did Diogenes say to the *First* Napoleon?
"Remove thy humpback shadow from my light."
Now History, who lies down at the feet of kings,
Whispers, the Conqueror had a crooked neck,
Which all his courtiers aped, but smoothes the hump
Clean off. Ha! I replace it, just as skill
Reclaims the lost, obliterated paintings
Of Rubens, Raphael, or the *not-mad* Blake.
You stare dazed. I, spectator of all facts,
Past, present, and future,—and I may remark
I never see your modern critics present
At Sinai, and such places that they prate
Of,—I hate shams, sir,—wring the neck off of
The history, cock, that would crow over me.
　　Col. (*Slinging paper down.*) "Your engine is to go
　　　　upon a bust!"
　　Dr. (*Grabbing paper and tearing it.*) A mocking spirit!
　　　　It serves me just right
For tarrying on the foot-hills, when I should
Be hastening to the peak — to Lilla Lamb.
　　Col. Oh! damn you to a thousand hells! You have
Torn up a whole life's labor.
　　Dr.　　　　　　　That? what is it?
　　　　(*With handkerchief over his eyes.*)
A dissertation on frog-soup? †
　　Col. (*Dashing off.*)　　　　　　*Frog hell.*

---

* *The Principles of Nature; her Divine Revelations and a Voice to Mankind*, by and through Andrew Jackson Davis, the Poughkeepsie Seer and Clairvoyant.
　† See Prefatory Note II.

ACT. III.

SCENE.— *The Apartments richly furnished and divided by folding doors. A glimpse of the mountains through the windows.*

Matilda Saunderson. (*Entering.*) The clergyman
    has come, — at home, ma'am?
Mrs. Willard. (*Going to mirror from window with
    papers in hand.*)   Yes.
Matilda. Your hair is disarranged. (*Fixes it.*)
Mrs. W. (*Stepping aside from the mirror indig-
    nantly.*)   Be quick.
Mr. Templeton. (*Entering and greeting Mrs. W.
    familiarly.*)   I know
My way — ha! —
    Mrs. W. There, there.   [*Matilda exit.*]
    Tempt.   As a horse his manger. —
How that young woman casts her eyes up! like
An angel floating down against her will.
    Mrs. W. I told her she should go to an oculist. —
What dreadful weather!
    Tempt.   Dust stood like a fog,
Impervious as South Carolina's jungles.
I must have pained you by my long delay.
    Mrs. W. Was at the General's speech, — I fancied you
Declaiming it.
    Tempt. Indeed!
    Mrs. W. (*Picking a toad up from the floor.*) Poor
    thing!
    Tempt.   A toad?
    Mrs. W. Poor George's study, pet.
    Tempt.   Pet!
    Mrs. W.   Never did
An old maid fondle a poodle more. You know
The frog renews his eye and limb when ruined; —

Tempt. Yes;—

Mrs. W. It and the hydra worm, in his opinion,
Are apices of nature whereon shines
The secret of existence, as upon
A mast in the dark mid sea, Saint Elmo's fire.

Tempt. And does he hope to light his foolish lamp
With such a fire?

Mrs. W. He cut its legs off twice,
And would have cut its eyes —

Tempt. Oh! —

Mrs. W. But for me.

Tempt. He thinks he can leap frog across all men,
Though they back one another to the skies
In rocky mountain ranges.

Mrs. W. Well, George says,
"Trip up the under men, the millions fall."

Tempt. How pitiable to behold a genius
Expiring dolphin-like, ēmitting brilliance, —
All hues except the brightest, Christian hope!
His brusqueness not a recent acquisition?
A genius is no genius save he show
Some eccentricity.

Mrs. W. No hypocrite,
Not he; no! no! He uses those horrid words
Because he notices the people, who
Would blush to mention them, as if all covered
Up by the glare of the dreadful opening furnace,
Shovel their fellow creatures into it,
Like so much coke or coal.

Tempt. Be not alarmed,
Dear,— no real fire.

Mrs. W. Where then does Satan abide?

Tempt. Indeed, dear, to be frank, we are not certain
That Satan is a personality,
(*Smiling.*) But soon intend to put it to the vote.

Mrs. W. If voted out, he may rebel, for is
Not, to rebel his nature?

Tempt.   Quite a wit.—
Been weeping ? Why, dear, why ?
    Mrs. W.   Oh ! when those lightnings
Were sweeping earth, as waves the deck of ship,
I saddened, thinking George must go so soon.
How good he was upon that other day
Of awfulest torrents, thunder ! Though all sopping
He would not change, — how could I urge him much ?
Moreover, I thought God would pity Emma,
Aleck, and me, and not let him take cold, —
But, like the lightning sped for latest news
Of darling — (*weeps.*)
    Tempt.   Better off.
    Mrs. W.   We meet here, love,
Clasp, and are sundered.
    Tempt. (*Checking himself quickly.*) Jane ! — too true !
        too true !
    Mrs. W. Nothing but woe, loss, pain.
    Tempt.   Pain has its virtues,
My dear. At birth, it wakens consciousness,
Our dormant faculties ; child, are not we
Now being born anew in Christ ? All pains
On earth arouse our consciousness of being
For glory, for are they that mourn not blesséd ?
Waken grand longings, faculties for Heaven,
Pinions that have not spreading room on earth.
    Mrs. W. Would that he had a tenth of Aleck's vigor,
Or father's !
    Tempt.   Or their earnest piety.—
Where is the General ?
    Mrs. W.   Out among the mountains.
    Tempt. Embodiments of Yankee go-a-head !
Ecstatic flights of land espying God
And, with all races, homewarding to Him ! —
Be frank, — why always sad ? One unacquainted
With your keen sensibility, might fancy,
Because of shadows often darkening you,

As from a cloud, or something you would fly from,
The cause of your distress, dear, must be *dreadful!*

Mrs. W. What! — Oh! shall tell you all — I do begrudge
My Emma to the Lord.

Tempt. Mere feeling, natural
Enough, dear. Who of us worth speaking of
But falls and lies a slab on a loved one's grave?
But you will not keep stubbornly averted
From graces, sent from Heaven to lift you up.
We must not live all root, but rise and blossom.

Mrs. W. God had so many angels, he could surely
Have spared me her. What had I ever done
For such affliction?

Tempt. Emma may have been
An anchor drawing your bright face from Him.

Mrs. W. So horribly disfigured by the fishes,
Aleck would let me have no glimpse of her,
No farewell kiss! Oh, it was horrible!

Tempt. Warmly He loves us, loves our lifted faces
So, that he turns their anchors into wings.

Mrs. W. I could not realize it in that light,
Hence, absent-heartedly, ran into wildest
Excesses, —

Tempt. No, no, no! —

Mrs. W. Of worldliness, —

Tempt. Oh! —

Mrs. W. From her madly ravishing memory;
Still, in each lovely child I saw her hooping,
Jumping the rope, or chirping infant games,
Swinging, or pouting, wondering, smiling, shouting,
So much so that one day — but it was wrong,
Oh, very wrong! — I clasped one to my heart,
Yes, felt like running off — I knew not whither —
Until I saw her mother wandering wild,
Like Jesus' mother on the three days' search.

Tempt. Oh, were such fervor but directed upward!
Remember Isaac was a response to prayer, — (*a knock.*)

Mrs. W. I think that you will like these purchases. —

Tempt. And John, whose *doubting* sire was stricken dumb.

Mrs. W. How even a few cents can make hundreds happy.

Tempt. (*Smiling.*) So thought Jehovah when he gave us five.

(*Matilda enters with a note which Mrs. W. reads.*)

Mrs. W. The General sends me word that he will meet
Us at the school, if possible.

Tempt.   Am glad
Of it.

Mrs. W.   Of what?

Tempt.   That he will meet us there.

[*Exit Mrs. W. through the folding doors, followed by Tillie who closes them.*]

Tempt. (*After taking the paper which Mrs. W. put on the table, and walking to and fro.*)

"We meet here, love, clasp, and are sundered."
Lord! how did I restrain? That was the moment.
Oh! how my lips burn feverish for one kiss,
My arms and breast for one embrace! I care
Not, care not, I will clasp her, come what will.
My love will out, though, like the genie freed
From casket, it cloud earth, push Heaven from sight.
But God! an Atlas now, I hold the heavens
Of millions; if I fall, what havoc! Verily,
A Heaven-quake, such as when bright Lucifer fell.
Oh! hers is such a whirlwind of a glance,
It carries every resolution off,
Dashes all sun-domed temples to the ground.
I *will* away, encounter it no more.
How weak, thou will of mine! Yet, what is pleasure
But hands across our eyes from ghastly death?
No wonder that our hands stick fast to them;
That only death, or Christ by miracle,
Has power to pull them down. How death, when drawing

Our bashful, maiden hands away, will grin,
And, with bone-crushing and ash-showering arms,
Embrace us! Oh! how help but rush from him
With eyes hand-pressed, as if by bird-shot stricken,
Or stone from sling! Stand, I will be no dastard,
But will pull down my hands, give death an eye
With which I could drag down the highest madman
To lick the dust. — Oh! he, a hero indeed,
Who runs the howling gauntlet of the world
Back to adjust what he has done amiss.
Though peremptory is Thy order, Thou
Most High! to do so, still how few — how few —
Oh! 'tis too much. If weeds, sown in the past,
Spring tall before us, will not firing them,
As we march on, suffice? This would I do
Most eagerly. (*Pauses, and Mrs. W. re-enters.*)
   How beautiful!
 Mrs. W.   The speech?
 Tempt. Youthful!
 Mrs. W.   Oh! — like the speech?
 Tempt.   Magnificent!
My carping mind is stricken like John's sire.
 Mrs. W. Repeat it.
 Tempt. With great pleasure — in the carriage.
From a high peak he points with glittering sword
At storming promontories, North and South,
The present ought to silence, bridge with peace.
       [*Exeunt Mrs. W. and Tempt.*]
 Matilda. (*Re-entering and shutting door.*)
I have a mind to try her purple on.
I thought the black owl, dozing on her face
For hours, flew off from the electric light
Of that good man's society. Is she
A moth around this candle of the Lord?
Could I get him at a seance, — Oh! — You! — Why?
 Ralph Raymond. (*Treading in softly*)
How have you fared, dear duck? — mean swan.

Matilda.   Caught something. —
Fouracres with his collar soaking —
  Ralph.   Fact
Is stranger than fiction; is he safe now?
  Matilda.   Yes.
Not cracked?
  Ralph. He tells the truth, confirmed by the Judge,
Whom, by the way, I hypnotised. The doctor —
Call him Empedocles, how grandiosely
He swells! like " peacock which," as Lilla sings,
" Appears, when tickled by your gaze, to think
The sunset, sunrise, only a paltry hen," —
Substantiates them. I have mesmerized
Our dear old gander, he will fly for miles,
Make stretching distance slink, coil, hibernate.
  Matilda. (*Slowly.*) The terror on Fouracres' face
       was surely
Too livid to have been a mere cosmetic.
  Ralph. A meteorite has fallen from the skies,
So large, bright, hot, that we will need no camp-fire,
Nor moon, for years. We need not now relieve
The doctor of his cash and disappear,
Except this fail.
  Matilda.   Salvation Plover! pshaw!
  Ralph. I have all carpet-bagged in case the scheme
Should leap the track, go down embankment.
  Matilda.   Madness!
Pshaw!
  Ralph. When so smart, adroit, in our chess-player, —
For Squigginson would swear it is the spirit
Of Templeton who drinks beer, bourbon, chews, and
       smokes, —
Plover will be no gawk in Willard's form;
If he should be, we skip. Come round at dusk.
      (*After listening a second Ralph escapes through
      the window, and Matilda, having turned the key
      in the door, closes the shutters. Great shaking and
      thumping at the door.*)

Matilda. Wait. (*Opens the door.*)
Col. (*Rushing in and searching about.*)
Where now hiding?
Matilda. Who?
Col. Fouracres.
Matilda. Hiding!
Why should he hide?
Col. I trailed him hither.
Matilda. Shall I call him?
Col. Whom were you just speaking to?
Matilda. Myself.
Col. You lie.
Matilda. Thank you. (*Starts.*)
Col. Stand. Why door locked? Where is he?
Matilda. With the General.
Col. Stupid thing! Did I not tell you that I trailed him hither?
Matilda. I do not know, then. May I ask the matter?
Col. No matter! — I shall teach him decency. The General feels unwell, will soon be here.
Matilda. Met Mrs. Willard?
Col. No, nor need we shock her;
A pin scratch at a distance seems to woman
A head off, or a body split in twain.
[*Exit, slamming the door.*]
Matilda. Has Plover spirit enough to animate
Great Willard's body? Every fibre, muscle,
Nerve? One or both arms will hang dead, I fear,
And so will head, both legs. — Preposterous! —
(*The shutters are shaken.*)
I hear him, go right back, go back. — What? You!
(*Terrified.*)
What brings you here?
Dr. (*Entering through window.*) Joy, hope, legs, levitation.

Matilda. (*Recovering.*) Where have you come from?
Dr. Lilla Lamb. Oh, glorious! Perfection!
Matilda. Not so loud.
Dr. All earth should hear.
Matilda. I hear the Colonel, — go.
Dr. At first my heart,
Like an enormous anchor, fell from me
Into the darkest depths, dragged me along,
Embedded me beneath dense miles of mud.
How could I think my engine, Grand Messiah,
Would start off at the cry of Lilla's infant?
Matilda. What! shocking! revolting! This shall not
    be. Do
You mind a dying girl's vagary? pshaw!
Dr. What are you pshawing at?
Matilda. Not much — your engine.
She says "that pain, Humanity's body-guard,
On picket duty to cry out 'to arms!'
At danger, would disband forever more;
That she would be the Joan of Arc to drive
The foe from earth," — DO you believe such raving?
I thought —
Dr. Think nothing since you can't think right. —
Matilda. A demon had false-lighted you, —
Dr. I am
No blind man, trusting to a dog for guidance.—
Matilda. To make of you, as he had made of Miller,—
Dr. I know the ring of truth, the thud of falsehood.—
Matilda. After Ascension muslin was all sold,—
Dr. Did I not tell my wife, it was good muslin —
"To put on the covers of my revelations?" —
Matilda. A public butt.
Dr. If I be butted, will
It not be by mere he-goats, for whose company
My nose has no desire?
Matilda. They come now, — go.
Dr. Was it to visit you that I came here?

Matilda. What will they think? (*Aloud.*) I have
 no money to spare
Sir, for the heathen in South — South — Cape of Good
 Hope.
Dr. (*Having indignantly stepped to the door.*)
Beware of an explosion that may shatter
The house to fragments, if he come in contact
With writeables,—pen, charcoal, chalk, or knuckle
Of howling debauchee, wild with the gout. (*Protected by
 a walking table.*)
Plover. (*Who has dashed at Dr.*)
Old devil you,—
 Col. (*Grabbing Plover fiercely.*)   Here, here.
 Plover. (*Dragging Col. without noticing him.*) Why
 cargo me
With a loose herd of fiends?
 Col. (*Plucking him fiercely.*)   Halt! • Damn you,
 quiet.
 Plover. Hello! Climbing upon my knee to drive?
The mule ain't hitched up yet.   You ought to warm
Your hands up, clap them on your shoulders, so. (*Breaks
 away.*)
 Col. Drag me a step or dash my hands in my face
Again, sir—
 Plover. Never saw you.
 Col. (*Enraged.*)   Liar!
 Plover. (*Sharply.*)   What?
 Col.   Liar!
 Plover. No more than you saw me when I first hailed
 you.
Don't you saccade me like a horse at brink, then.
This is a rough and tumble with me down
Just long enough.
 Col. (*To Matilda.*) A carriage?
 Matilda. (*Returning from window.*) Mrs. Willard.
 Ralph. (*Entering, to Dr.*) Mild, then unmanageable,
 like the Duke.*

* New York Sun.

Col. (*To Plover.*) Lie on the lounge. (*Pushes him toward it.*)

Judge. (*Surprised at the Dr.'s presence.*) You here?

Dr. Only a cracked
Philosopher — who, when he sheds his senses,
His brains, stops not, but rushes faster ahead
In blatherskiting, having got more light, —
Can doubt the fact.

Judge. How? how?

Ralph. (*Loud-voiced.*) An angel, eagling
Down, grabs you pup-like by the hair — this wise —
And lifts —

Judge. Oh! Oh! what are you doing?

Ralph. Showing
You 'tis no joy to travel through the air
When spirits make a handle of your hair;
Envy no prophet, genius, his broad ken,
Thus is he lifted o'er his fellow-men. —
Need me for consultation, doctor?

Dr. Stay.

Plover. I want a drink, am dry as blazes.

Col. Can
Not have it now.

Plover. Can't hey?

Col. No.

Judge. Templeton,
Is coming.

Plover. Is, hey? Rum is too good-looking
A gal to be long left upon the shelf.
You bet that preacher takes a smack in tunnels.

Col. Hush.

Plover. You will know me next time Sis, — but, gosh!
How goes it? Smouch me whiskey.

Tillie. (*Pinched, screeching.*) Oh! Oh!

Tempt. (*Entering.*) Ha!

Col. What are you screeching for? get spreads and pillows.

Judge. (*To Mrs. W., entering.*) Bear the affliction which the Lord is pleased —

Tempt. Your dark presentiment is but too true.
Tillie. (*Pushing Mrs. W. back.*)
I will not let her in — no, never will —
Till I tell all.
 Tempt.   Ha!
 Mrs. W.   Let me go.
 Tillie.   No, never
'Till I breathe out the torture choking me.
 Mrs. W. (*Breaking through.*)
What matters your sore throat to me?
 Tillie.   Then go.
            [*Exit.*]
 Mrs. W. (*Tearing off bonnet and rushing toward Plover.*)
Poor Aleck! what can ail him? Aleck! Aleck!
Does he not know me? how he stares!
 Judge. (*Pointing to Plover's head and shaking his own.*)   Come, dear.
 Mrs. W. What? No, it cannot be,— Aleck, one word!
 Judge. (*Bending over to Tempt. and whispering.*)
Crush into softest sand her stony way. —
 Mrs. W. What have we done to be afflicted thus?
 Tempt. (*Leading Mrs. W. aside.*)
God's holy will is an enigma, dear,
Which He alone can open, which we tangle
The more, the more we thumb and finger it;
For who can grasp the thousand cords? or one?
At most, we catch but threads whereby too often
We hang ourselves, protruding blackest tongues
At Heaven, or bind ourselves in the dark and smother.
 Mrs. W. Oh! that my mind, my life, not his, were—
  Oh!
I saw all this, his forehead gushing red,
His eyes blood-blind, his wan hands wandering.
 Judge.   What!
 Mrs. W. (*Rushing back to Plover.*)
Aleck! Of course he knows me, — Aleck!
 Col. (*Leading her back.*)   Come.

Tempt. Ere having been eight minutes in the carriage,
She sprang up as deranged, exclaiming, "Lord!
Lord! home! drive home, my husband bleeds, is dying." *
    Judge. Oh, Jephthah! Oh! Oh!   [*Exit Ralph.*]
    Mrs. W.   How his hands go round
(*Half suppressed.*) As though a — fool!
    Dr.   Compare them rather, madame,
With those of God creating the spheres of light.
    Plover. Light? Engine not to burst?
    Dr.   Oh!
    Mrs. W.   Conscious, — Aleck!
(*Rushes toward Plover but is instantly drawn away by
                         Col.*)
    Dr. I thought the lady carped at the spirit's method.
    Plover. (*Singing.*)

        My daddy was a cobbler, whom
        The Lord had given a soul;
        "Dip, dip," says he, "your crust of gloom
        Into the sparkling bowl;
        Make, make it soft as wedding cakes,
        For Oh! A big galoot you,
        To crack your teeth, then howl with aches,"
           (*Presses his cheeks with his hands.*)
        "Till 'tis delight to boot you,
        To crack your teeth, then howl with aches.
           (*Shakes his head violently.*)

    Mrs. W. Physicians — where are they?
    Col.   We have the greatest
The West can boast of, Dr. Squigginson.
    Mrs. W. What ails him?
    Dr. (*Abstracted.*)   Ma'am?
    Mrs. W.   What?
    Dr.   Ma'am?
    Mrs. W.   What ails him?
    Dr. Beg pardon for a moment, am receiving
A telegram now from bloody Mars.
    Tempt.   What!
    Mrs. W.   Oh! —

       * Robert Dale Owen.

Dr. A telegram, pulsation on left temple.
I am informed this case is much sublimer
Than the Grand Duke's, though Patsy is —
    Col.   No matter! —
    Dr. (*To Col.*) The only spirit that has boarded
        him, (*Pointing to Plover.*)
The other in the vision in the tent, —
    Col. What shall we *now do?* —
    Dr.   Having been prophetic.
    Mrs. W.   (*Looking from Dr. to Col.*)
This man a doctor?
    Col.   None in all the land
Is better for this case.
    Tempt.   Strange!
    Col.   Would one, sceptical
As I am, trust in a charlatan?
    Tempt.   Frost cuts
Grotesquer capers on our intellects
Than on our panes and eaves.
    Mrs. W.   Fetch him upstairs.
    Judge. 'Twas terrible trouble to get him ho —
        home.
    Mrs. W. This is too hard to lie on.
    Dr.   Nonsense, madam!
A soft bed were too lofty for his breeding;
He'd take the feathers out to get inside.
    Plover. Herrings for breakfast, —
    Col.   Thinks he is a sot,
Though would this were his murkiest vagary! —
    Plover. Like Richy who went begging for a nip
From Lazarus.
    Col.   He's been of late imbibing
Too much religion. He must be weaned off
With doses ever lessening — mean increasing.
    Tempt. The horrors?
    Plover. (*Springing with gyrating arms at Templeton,
        who, to avoid being struck, frequently dodges.*)
        Horrors of you, by jingo!

Mrs. W. Aleck!
Col. Here.
Judge. Lord!
Plover. When Nature blundered, did not give
You a big pole for a nose —
Col. (*Plucking Plover back.*) Hush! —
[*Ralph re-enters.*]
Plover. (*Breaking from Colonel and Judge.*)
Forty footer —
To constantly swing around you, "*Clear the track*"
Being on it in black or scarlet print,
As she gives rattles to those things that always
Go belly-whoppers, —
(*Is pulled back toward the lounge by the Colonel, the Judge, the Dr., and Ralph, the last volleying raps, at which Mrs. W., Tempt., and the Judge are startled.*)
Mrs. W. Aleck!
Tempt. Pitiful! —
Plover. Why not have gumption enough to add the alarm?
(*To Col.*) You yallar-jandered, pumpkin-headed fool!
(*Plover seizes, lifts, and is about to dash to the ground the Colonel, who has pinched him.*)
Judge. Down burst the sand-storms and the walls collapse!
Mrs. W. (*To Col.*) How rough! stop this! I will not have it.
Col. (*Released by Ralph, Plover remembering his position.*) There's
For gentleness! I must have my own way,
Or I shall leave him as he is. Away, Jane!
False sympathy is deadlier far than hatred.
Mrs. W. If dead, he were in Heaven, and I were happy.
Judge. Oh!
Mrs. W. Head-gashed Hector, after the wheels of —
life, —
Oh! Oh! Release him, Father Almighty!

Judge. (*Clasping her.*)   Oh!
Would you be happier, Jane, if he were — dead?
  Col. (*Pushing him towards Plover.*) Poor father takes
    it ill. (*To Judge.*) Help me to hold him.
  Mrs. W. Emma, then Aleck, — but it cannot be, —
  Ralph. The Duke, at presence of his wife, grew furi-
    ous —
  Mrs. W. Aleck, your father writes he will be here
To-morrow, — but, O God! it is! it is! (*Weeps and ges-
    tures wildly.*)
  Dr. (*To Col.*) Persuade her to retire, for he needs
    rest.
  Tempt. He speaks of snakes, the horrors, verily.
  Col. You might have called it crapulence.
  Tempt.   Why?
  Col.   Nothing.
  Tempt. Noth —
  Col.   Being a soldier, he was bayoneted
When you hit Jane with the butt-end, such harsh lan-
    guage.
(*Leading Mrs. W. to Tempt.*) Come, 'tis the Doctor's
    positive injunction.
  Mrs. W. I will not leave him.
  Col.   Come, come. (*Folds the doors.*)
  Tempt. (*Conducting her through them.*) Come, my
    dear.
How stand this longer? Shall I go for doctors?
  Mrs. W. What! yes, do! do! A dozen, at least. Poor
    Aleck!
Never more sprightly than this morning, when
He cantered from my proud and happy vision,
Like yellow-bird, to come back never more.
  Tempt. Let not your pain, my dear, be too acute; —
Men overjoyed, cut saturnalian antics; —
I have not now the fear I had at first.
I would suggest, —
  Mrs. W.   What?
  Tempt.   I should not, perhaps; —
  Mrs. W. Why not? do! do!

Tempt. Since I let slip the hint,
May be I ought; still, Jane, it pains, —
 Mrs. W. What is it?
 Tempt. Oh! had not God just freshened me with grace
To start anew in the race, as Paul describes it,
I scarcely could have reached the resolution
To hint remotely that if, now and then,
You would with glances sweep out nooks and corners,
You might find dust.
 Mrs. W. Be plain.
 Tempt. Matilda *may* be
Pure.
 Mrs. W. Nonsense!
 Tempt. Then you know she is not pure?
 Mrs. W. I did not say so.
 Tempt. Was her action — pushing
You back — not queer? I thought she had some dreadful
Confession.
 Mrs. W. (*Contemptuously.*) Oh!
 Tempt. Well, I hope so.
 Mrs. W. How you frighten!
 Tempt. I know how penitents are prone to act,
Tear all considerations, bandages,
From their gashed foreheads, though they bleed to
 death.
Breathe not what I have hinted, but be watchful.
 Mrs. W. Hurry the doctors, please. [*Exit Temp.*]
 (*Shaking the door.*) George! George!
 Col. (*Unfolding them.*) What? — where
Is Templeton?
 Mrs. W. Gone after doctors.
 Col. What!
Does he care for the General more than we do?
 Mrs. W. It seems he does.
 Col. Not till the filmy ailment
On Aleck's eyes is off, — the seance — when?
 Dr. (*Starting.*) What seance? Think that I would
 stay to be
At a scene of murder?

Col. Hell and damnation!
Mrs. W. George!
Col. Approach him not.
Mrs. W. You must be silly. (*Rushes towards Plover.*)
Col. (*Plucking her back.*) Not
For your own easement but for his. His wound,
Far more than yours, will needlessly be probed,
Kept red, raw, gaping, not let heal, form skin.
Ralph. (*At door, with hand on head, and to Dr.*)
A telegram directs you to remain.
Mrs. W. Oh!
Col. Where is the girl? She did not fetch the spreads.
[*Exit, kicking over the chairs in his way and locking the door.*]
Mrs. W. Quick! I insist on a dozen, at least.
(*Pulls the bell violently, then instinctively arranges the chairs.*)
Dr. Insane, ma'am.
Mrs. W. Why not have other physicians to consult with?
Dr. Their chattering sickened me at Petersburg.
The Duke was raging, raving, swearing that
He was a carpenter, — nay, Nihilist, —
Wanted to work. Materialistic quacks,
Who would have us look down upon the ground,
As were we villains going to the gallows,
And not aloft to Him, who scatters suns
To draw our eyes from filth, our starving birds
From adders, venomous worms, came in a mob,
Shook shoulders, heads, then turned on him their broken
Backs, humped with pride, swift-deserting dromedaries,
Each, all opining that he should be smothered
Between two ticks.
Mrs. W. Good Lord! Did he get cured?
Dr. Can it be possible you do not know?
Mrs. W. I now recall it faintly, — really cured?
Dr. Would I palm off a falsehood on the world,
Give the poor savage sawdust for best meal?

Mrs. W. I do not think you would; still, I know nothing
About you. Father! George! George! Aleck! Aleck!
(*The table moving, she rushes from one door to the other,
    then drops. Patsy appears, has pig's head in one hand,
    and with the other he takes flowers and vegetables from
    his bosom and flings them on Mrs. W.*)
  Dr. A mere leaf-stirring breeze from Summer-land. —
Cease! heartless, cruel —
  Patsy. (*Eating the pig's head.*) My instructions is
To soften brains with every kind of pounder, —
Dirt-rooted, dewy flowers that bloom afar —
Noises, and fun.* I likes to have a racket,
For it recalls my youth and Donnybrook.†
  Dr. Begone! I know you by your odor — off,
You skunk!
  Patsy. No skoonk am I, but Irishman;
And divil another save me shadow can
Be found in hell.
  Dr. (*Smiling.*) That lacks the golden ring,
Which Truth puts on the finger of our hearing,
His bride. Begone! ‡
  Patsy. Pat, in the tint, your rousin;
But when the war is done, begone, you skoonk!
  Dr. Subject yourself to moral suasion, Patrick.
Great Britain says, "you never can."
  Patsy. (*Tossing furniture and so forth.*) Phew! freedom
For iver! iver! Down with all such foineries,
Fit only to be frill-frolls of fat Blazes, —
The red-haired divil that will dance herself
Down at the whole world's wake. Poor, blading sowls
Are pinned right through their hearts on thim; ay, joost
Like butterflies in the case in Cintral Park.

---

* The dark spirit Patsy told Mr. Henry Kiddle that he came for fun.
† Professor A. R. Wallace.
‡ We have the testimony of Mr. Andrew Jackson Davis that the Diakka, the unprogressed spirit, is known by the smell.

Dr. You have a noble heart   Bow down to reason:
Let Reason, with her pearl-set crown of gold,
Now temperate-zone your head.
   Patsy.   I will surrinder.
Forgive me, for on earth it was me habit
To soften brains, I being — Oh! Oh! Oh!
   (*Clenches his fists, grinds his teeth, and stamps in fury.**)
   Dr. A burglar?
   Patsy.   Nor.
   Dr.   An atheist?
   Patsy.   Worse! an atheist,
Being sinsare, go straight to Hiven, without
Having to pay a tole, or being sarched
By Fire, the custom-house official, that
Will lave none smuggle a joy beneath their oxther.
   Dr. What were you?
   Patsy. (*Falling on face.*)   One that taught the divil
      villany.
   Dr. Then you must be Archbishop —
   Patsy. (*Leaping up in a rage and flinging the pig's head
      at the doctor.*)   Phew! no *bishop!*
Oh! oh! why pull the scab from such a sore?
Pull half out a wild, slumbering tooth, that niver
Can be extracted from me jaw?   Oh! Oh!
Break over again me arms and legs, joost set?
   Dr. Excuse me, brother; I will not again
Commit the blunder.   Please produce credentials.
   Patsy. (*Retiring.*)   I have St. Michael here for riference;
Aaron will recommend me as tip-top,
And Moses, too, will give me a chara*c*ter,

---

* It occupied less than an hour in the writing, and some of the words the spirit seemed to be unable to emphasize strongly enough by heavy and repeated underscoring; as when the word "*archbishop*" was written it appeared that he could not heap ignominy enough upon it, — striking at it with a pencil, and thus defacing it. . . . . . She seemed to see him grinding his teeth, clenching his fists, and wildly gesticulating, in the anguish of contrition, and in the deepest hatred of the things he denounced — most of all himself. — *Henry Kiddle.*

Or any other thing I am in need of;
For we are now fast freends, — go arm in arm.
Show me your freends, I'll tell ye what ye are.
(*Changes his attire.*) I am the trumpeter; he spakes the truth.
(*Rushes forward, with yellow wings outspread and bottle to mouth.*) Aaron am I; there, feel my rod. (*Kicks him, retires and instantly returns garmented like a Rabbi, with bottle on head.*)
Dr. Oh! Oh!
Patsy. Horned Moses, I.
Dr. (*Searchingly.*) What would you tell the world?
Patsy. That spirits are no more a set of liars.*
Dr. Good news!
Patsy. Why fetch ye bad? This is the bishop.
I biled and thin clamshelled him, till no bristle
Of superstition did I lave on him
From tail to jowl.
    Dr. (*Turning aside.*) Still I am doubtful. Oh!
    Patsy. (*Having bitten his ear.*) That I am rale my teeth will testify.†
    Dr. Oh! for the test of the moral worth of spirits.
How would you treat the Scarlet Woman, whom
The bull-like future is to horn and hoof
To pieces?
    Patsy. Let me at her!
    Dr. Glorious!
    Patsy. You
Play her, — with pleasure show you, — break my crozier
Upon her skull. (*Strikes him.*)
    Dr. Oh! Oh!
    Patsy. Whist! sure it's pleasure
To feel a crack intended for a foe.
I'll be no future, be no bull a backing,
And backing, till 'twill find itself off dock. (*Chases and strikes him.*)
    Dr. Oh, cease! cease! Reason, unadulterated
With thumps, hard husks for swine, I much prefer,

---

* Mr. Kiddle.   † Mr. Davis, *Diakka.*

Having a god-like mind; yet must remember
You were a bishop; hence, far more at home
In thumping than in ratiocination.
Why have you come?
    Patsy.   To offer me services,
To do the honors, to uncork the rite,
If you will lave me, — and if you will not,
Why, do the other thing — do the tinpanning.   [*Patsy
    disappears.*]
    Dr. (*After hesitating.*) If there be any rite, assuredly.
Uncork the rite, as characteristic of
A wine-imbibing hypocrite, as blossoms
Upon the nose. His basting me so hard
Through fear I might misapprehend his meaning,
Puts his sincerity beyond a doubt.
(*Feeling his ear.*) Which was it, he or Moses, bit my ear?
    (*Extricates Mrs. W. who has stirred.*)
You will not mind these manifestations, madam,
When used to them; mere flies of Summer-land,
Now thickening on old broken-winded Time,
Near his last kick. Unfortunately, madam,
Coarse earthly traits most stubbornly adhere, —
We have to crush huge rocks to get their gold.
    (*Patsy, French-capped and liveried, re-enters, and,
    after drinking from the bottle, fills a glass, which
    the doctor takes and gives to Mrs. W., having seat-
    ed her. After pausing a minute, she drinks.*)
    Patsy. (*Before a mirror.*) Is it the master, mistress, is
    afeerd
That strangers will judge too much by the looks,—
Will think the stiff, foin fellow in the sate
Behind, with folded arms, and niver driving,
Is the big-bug himself? and the young woman,—
Complected like the crimson-globed lime water
In drug shops lit, — in whose arms squales the babby,
With flowing white dress, being a hivenly comet,
Who but the mother? Does the one in front
Think babbies are a dangerous, new invintion,

Not to be touched, neared? — hence, that folks may not
Swallow the wrong dose, on the man and maid
Is labelled, *pison*. Down with all such pison!
(*Tears cap and coat off, dances on them with vengeance, snatches the wine the Dr. is about to drink, swallows it* and disappers.*)
Dr. If spirits be vulgar, be not scandalized,
Madam, but bask in the pleasure sure to shine
From culture.
    Mrs. W. (*Faintly, and gazing about.*) Where am I?
Lord! in my own house? (*Listens.*)
Father! George! George!
    Judge. (*Unfolding the doors, and wildly staring about.*)
My —
    Mrs. W. (*Repelling him.*) Go away from me.
    Judge. What!
    Mrs. W. Aleck! Aleck!
    Judge.   Oh! look! I can not. (*Points to window.*)
    Mrs. W. What!
    Judge. (*To Dr.*) Look from window!
    Mrs. W.   Is he dashed to atoms?
    Judge. He verily is.
    Mrs. W.   My darling husband!
    Ralph. (*Returning from window.*)   No,
Madam; no.
    Judge.   He entreated piteously
For cordials.
    Ralph.   I beheld him entering Mars.
Stentorian voices —
    Judge.   I could not refuse him. —
    Ralph. Shouted " Oh! flowery-arch the way for Willard,
Who put rebellion, the forest-fire, out."—
    Judge.   Hearing
Those noises, I thought he had broken loose,
So sought for George to help. —
    Ralph.   " Hail to our chief!"
    Dr. As in the vision in the tent exactly!
As I have been informed by telegram.

         * William Howitt.

Mrs. W. Were he deranged, you never would have left him.
Judge. I left him in this person's charge.
Mrs. W. (*Contemptuously.*) Oh!
Ralph. Madam,
I go; I stay not where I am mistrusted. (*Starts.*)
Dr. (*Following a few steps.*)
Dispatches crowd now, Ralph, from Moses, Aaron,
Bacon, Confucius, that the snow, light, *has*
To fall to-night and cover the whole world up;
That I will read minds, souls, combine them rightly,
Felicitously.
Ralph. Glorious! glorious! I
Will sound the tocsin press, awaken the world! [*Exit.*]
Mrs. W. (*After staring at the Dr. and Ralph.*)
Neither is in the house, — Oh! horrible!
Bar every door against that vampire, serpent
That wound around me with her slimy grin.
Judge. My darling, —
Mrs. W. Do not darling me.
Judge. What!
Mrs. W. Never
More! never more! A father, brother, — but
It cannot be, — nor Aleck, — but 'tis, 'tis! —
O God! I cry for scalding, scarring vengeance, —
On all who have abetted her as well,—(*Judge staggers.*)
And must it be in vain, as when I cried
For my poor darling, whom the crabs were eating,
The eels were boring holes through? Oh! Oh!
Judge. (*To Dr.*) Off!
Begone, sir!
Dr. What is this?
Judge. Depart at once.
Col. (*Dashing in.*) What were you yelling about?
Judge. Have you him now
In custody?
Mrs. W. (*Her fit coming on.*) Quick! if you love me, tell

Me where he is! I will forgive all, never
Allude to this.
   Col.   Who?
   Judge.   Aleck.
   Col. (*Breaking from Mrs. W.*) What!
   Dr.   Good-day.
   Col. Stand!
   Dr.   I have been requested to withdraw.
   Mrs. W. (*Rending collar for air.*)
Oh, that this were her heart, soul, mind, life! — *Oh!*
              (*Drops in an epileptic fit.*)
   Judge. My darling! can I gyve you to the stake?
No! no! (*Col. pushes Judge aside.*)
   Col. Has fainted, must have water, air.
          (*Carries Mrs. W. toward the window.*)
   Judge. (*To Dr.*) *Fly from our sight!*
   Dr. The lady needs my skill. (*Opens the window.*)
   Judge. (*Falling on knees.*) Supreme Jehovah! if with-
      in Thy breast
There be one jot of pity, stay my arm,
Or, with a streak of lightning shiver, shiver
My knife and me; but harm no hair of her.

ACT IV.

SCENE. — *The Apartments as at the end of preceding Act.*

   Col. (*Snapping.*) Those who have dogmas, who have
      heads off in
The keeping of somebody else, on ice,
Ought never to touch Science.
   Judge.   Ha! ha! ha!
What! leave it to you idiots, iron-bound
In the conceit that with your hand, five senses,
You can grasp, not alone the whole creation,

But every possibility, — squeeze all
To nothing? Such a clammy hand at that!
    Col. (*Fiercely.*) Will one expert not overbalance millions, —
    Judge. You reaped the pumpkin, you were served just right. —
    Col. Though these be scientific geniuses,*
Be Newtons, as one spark, a magazine?
    Judge. Spark, go not out! the pack of future glories
Will not crack off, if you go out, O Punk!
Does earth contain but one expert? that, *you?*
Creation has not standing room for two
With such big feet as yours, — must widen out.
What a great loss to the world, your death! ha! ha!
Fool! fool!
    Col. Some men are like Niagara, sir,
Great in their fall; I have not fallen yet. —
Why toss your hands up to to the blind Unknowable?
You might have carried Jane to the godlier breeze.
    Judge. Oh! like an old oak, I was split by lightning
Into the widest supplicating arms,
Arms never more to fold in flourishing peace.
    Col. Since you know this, gulp it from thought. Why chew
The pill, as cow with swinging jaws, her cud?
    Judge. Know what?
    Col. That supplicants are sundered trees,
Fit only to be fuel.
    Judge. Know no such thing.
    Col. Wood split for hell must go there, else cold angels
Would quarrel to get closer to the heaters.
    Judge. (*Tremblingly.*) Add not impiety, or that may touch
The avalanche of Heaven, send it down crashing
Upon our heads, sir!
    Col.   Let it crash.

* Dr. G. M. Beard, " Psychology of Spiritism," in *North American Review.*

Judge. Tut, tut!
Fools they who climb a tree, the lightning's lair,
To shake their puny fists at Heaven.
  Col. Could clutch
Your stupid throat.
  Judge. No doubt you could, you murderer!
Oh! when a tempest dashes in your breast,
How help some splashing out in speech? how help
The lightnings flashing out, when thunder clouds
Are clashing in your poor, old, bursting brain?
  Col. Hush! that will do.
  Judge. That will not do. I could
Have flattened my poor head in an iron vice,
When you, as well as he now off, loud laughing
At us — big idiots! fools! — and that grim wizard
Who left this house in ruins — behold the wreck! —
Pelted in me the direst of explosives.
  Col. Big idiot, fool, to not have gone pathfinder
Myself! If you had followed in my steps,
We never would have tumbled down the gulch,
Nor have to climb up glacier on the slide.
  Judge. Oh! had she only passed away! had never
Opened her eyes again on wretched me,
The Brocken Shadow on the peak of Hell!
God! she is all charred black with jealousy.
  Col. That damned, old preacher! — but he may be
    worked.
  Judge. Why — O you idiot! —
  Col. Hush, I say. —
  Judge. Did you
Slam-bang the door — shaking the house — in the girl's
Face?
  Col. I could choke that screecher. Was not Jane
About to slam it?
  Judge. Where get help now? where?
The coachman and the nurse next door have fled.
  Col. May have eloped, — what is there strange in
    that?
  Judge. Matilda knew too much to be slammed out.

Col. Guess a few cents will bandage her resentment.
Judge. I hope so. Why did you haul Templeton
Back?
Col. (*In derision.*) Why! why! why!
Judge. Yes, *why?*
Col. (*Sharply.*) To quench the fuse
Crawling to powder mountaining around us.
Judge. Yet did not quench it, for is he not summoning
Doctors in spite of your entreaties?
Col. Never
Entreated him, nor any one.
Judge. You should have. —
God! did you say —
Col. *Say what?*
Judge. My mind is wandering, —
Col. I might have said that often. —
Judge. O you snarling
Young pup! how you delight in showing off
Your foolish teeth!— that Templeton is to witness
The doctor at the operation?
Col. Yes.
Judge. Crazy?
Col. On your account and Jane's. My conscience
Needs no Caligula pontoon, or bridge,
To cross the rapids of the foggy future.
Judge. Ha!
Col. Being impulsive, he will, if requested
At seance to perform the ceremony,
Comply.
Judge. After so gross an insult? nonsense!
Since Plover has absconded, had we better
Not instantly secure the body, fetch
It home?
Col. No, can't. When they were spading the grave,
Oil spouted from the ground, as geyser from whale,
And, like a harpoon, darted the lightning.
Judge. Lord!
Col. The irritated, crimson monster rose

Sublimely, swallowed Willard and the horse,
And is now drawing the forest down its throat.
   Judge. Where the retrenchment?
   Col.   None; we must advance.
If all be lost, here is my panacea. (*A pistol.*)
   Judge. Oh! All along I fancied I could lead
Poor Jane to a last adieu. Fool! — Where is Plover
Now? Where? Where?
   Col. With Fouracres stacked, I guess.
   Judge. You will not now shout, "Damn your hope so,"
    — will you?
   Col. But for your damned stupidity —
   Judge.   My what?
   Col. Your damned stupidity —
   Judge.   Yes, I deserve this, —
   Col. He would be here. —
   Judge.   I fathered one so stupid,
He roomed his sister with a maniac.
   Col. No fool to let a maniac escape.
   Judge. How now procure the wretches? how procure
    them?
   Col. They are in league with Squigginson, that's cer-
    tain.
Both will be loaded, and at hand, when wanted.
   Judge. Are wanted now.
   Col.   That fool-fraud will not quicken
His gait for any consideration; got
Indignant at a proffer of some cash.
He speaks of nothing but his damned, old engine,
Which I a thousand times have wished in hell.
   Judge. Oh! may be they show law our trail, and blood-
    hounds,
With wide mouths, sniffle the air. Whither for refuge?
" Depart from me forever, thou accursed!
Sit, toad-like, in thy rocky deed forever."
O George, George! —
   Col.   Hush! —
   Judge.   Come, come! and throw ourselves

Before a sister, child ; unbosom all,
Though earthquake billows of the blackest ocean,
And crave forgiveness.
   Col. (*Breaking away.*) Pshaw !
   Judge.   Cling, cling to her,
The angel, wrench the blessing from her grasp.
   Col. Such notions, clogging shoes, must be slung off,
For we must go barefoot, like white-heeled lightning,
If we would keep ahead of the avalanche,
Whose shadow creaps before us like a river.
No time to give our private feelings quarter,
They must be routed, slain, if they obstruct
Or barricade our Country's way to weal.
Do I, as well as you, not have to storm ?
Do I forget how that vile rascal lifted
Me bull like, was about to dash me down ?
No ; but such feelings must be handed over
To Memory, nurse who will go sleep with them,
Nor waken 'till the sunshine warms their faces.
   Judge. For Heaven's sake wash your hands not, for you make
Me think of Pilate. Even were Plov — he here,
The rite, without her free, full-eyed volition,
Were null, though Gabriel should perform it.
   Col.   Would
I have this marriage consummated ?
   Judge.   What ?
   Col. Love Jane too much for that. I have arranged,—
   Judge. Lord ! then the lightning strikes the knife.
      That voice
Was not satanic, as I half suspected
When you became its advocate. George, George,
Forgive me for my ghastliest opinion
Of you, no true reflection of your face,
But picture taken on a cloudy day, —
Which all my life so far has been. Yet how —
   Col. Oh ! during the conflict I could turn the grape
From enemy to talkers in the rear.

When we have taken the high-bluffed battery,
We then can talk, wipe perspiration off,
The thoughts and feelings big upon our brows.
 Andrew. (*Entering and presenting cards.*)
De doctors, —
 Col. Tell them that they are too late.
 Andrew. I did, but dey got huffed at being fooled.
Two handed me dese bills.
 Col.   Show them to the door.
Tell Squigginson I want him instantly.
          [*Exit Andrew.*]
 Judge. I'll not attend the seance; I need rest.
 Col. Quick to your room and sleep.
 Judge.   Sleep is an eyelid
Torn from my eyes. Would it were fastened down! —
(*Turning on Col.*) No doubt you would, base ingrate!
 Col.   What?
 Judge.   Wish it
Were tightened down, like coffins.
 Col.   Did not say so.
 Judge. You meant it; I can hear your muttering
  heart.
God! is to be a parent not to have
The pangs of child-birth every day we live?
Oh! well for those delivered of their pangs.
I now were happy but for Jane, —
 Col.   Be quicker.
Racing with snails to beat them just a neck? —
 Judge. And who will say she will not be a Goneril?
           [*Exit.*]
 Col. Hell! he will be the devil to wield. Would he
Were scabbarded by Nature, put aside!
What slashing, glittering use for him now? none. —
Oh, helpless infants in that juggler's arms!
Yes, my long fasting to starve out and silence
Disease, which storms from heights impregnable,
  (*Patsy appears and hops about toad-wise.*)
Is, to the scientist, an explanation

Of dreams as vivid as realities. (*Turns aside.*)
Oh, that I were a god for just one minute!
These dogs, that bite the world and set it into
Convulsions, would be brained.
> (*Patsy hops over him as in leap-frog, then out.*)
>
> Brain fever! opium!
Horrors! dementia! anything that's rational! —
But this a time for drilling thoughts, reviewing?
Yet one must put his men in line ere battle,
Must pre-arrange a masterly retreat.

> *Judge.* (*Rushing in.*) Oh, it is terrible! I cannot stay
Alone, — I will not. Steps came after me,
And a loud voice said, —

> *Col.* (*Pushing the Judge out.*) Damn these voices! go.
> *Judge.* I wash my hands of this, George! On your head,
Not mine, the blood. I said he verily is. [*Exeunt both.*]

> *Patsy.* (*Reappearing with hats, coats, breeches, and a straw bed, which he rips, and out of them making two figures,* which he placards Vice and Slavery.*)

Patsy, my b'y, since you are a good hand
At bishop, joost now try your hand at hangin'
All divils. Pulpits, shinin' doors of Hiven,
Are divils' gibbets, too, which is why you
Should hang thim. Kin do it — as well as Squiggins.—
Quick, doctor! or I'll lave you none to strangle. —

> (*Hangs Vice and Slavery on the door.*)

Me b'y, act marchants, owners of fact'ries, mines,
And tin'ments, — Black-holes! — who, with indignation
Are flame-faced, as their blood drinched coal, — hang Slavery
In if'gy; but noose not your nick in fun,
Least starving thousands pluck the rope and run.

(*Pulls the rope and runs out, slamming the door. Ralph Raymond enters, constructs the cabinet, then puts the gas-jets at the point of flaring. The Dr. and Smith Van Doozer enter with the sheeted Redcem-*

---

* Dr. Phelps.

er, welcomed with lively music, to which the gas-
jets dance.*)
 Dr. (Letting the redeemer drop, and cutting down the
effigies.) We hang themselves now ; aye, till black
and pulseless.
All that the Churches, Reformations, States,
Codes, Revolutions, have accomplished, is
To gibbet these monsters, fiends, in effigy.
 (Throws the figures out, and then lifts the machine.)
 Van Doozer. With such conclusions how remain a
deist?
 Dr. (Letting the redeemer drop.)
There is a God ; I know there is. Law, beauty, —
Behold them! beauty, the blushing consciousness
Of Nature at the presence of her Maker ;
And law, the falling into line of forces
Beholding their Commander. — Smith Van Doozer,
What are you shaking your head at? got the palsy?
 Van Doozer. (Having smiled, and nodded negatively
several times, a habit of his when disapproving.)
Shaking the sand of your surging rhetoric
Out of my ears.
   (Enter Mrs. Squigginson and Mrs. Lamb.)
 Dr.   Ha!
 Mrs. S.   Will you not defer
Your arguing, please, till after the Savior's coming?
When there will be no need of it, thank Heaven!
(Complying, they move the redeemer toward the cabinet.)
 Col. (Dashing in.) Thunder and lightning! who the
devil are these?
Out!
 Dr. Friends.
 Col.   What business here?
 Dr. (Smiling.)   To be the ballast
In our balloon.
 Col. Dash out the sand-bags, go

    * Mr. Tyndall.

The faster up.
 Mrs. S.   Might strike against the sky!
 Dr. (*Abstractedly fingering Mrs. S.'s hair.*)
What truth in the interjections of a child!
Most crashingly do we impinge our heads
Against the sky, when we precipitate
A fellow-creature from a flying good;
Cries out the thunder; "Cain, where is thy brother?"
 Col. Order them out, or I will pitch them out.
 Van D. (*Approaching Col.*) If you cry "pitcher," son-
  ny, I cry "lick."
 Dr. "Do to another nothing which you would
Not have him do to you," says St. Confucius.
 Col. Confucius be damned! all out — this way.
 Judge. (*Rushing to the engine.*) Who — who upon
  the stretcher? Is it Jane?
 Col. No, no!
 Judge.   Lord! can it then be Aleck?
 Col.   No.
 Judge. I must see — *I must see!*
 Dr. (*Grabbing him.*)   Hands off! not death!
But life.
 Col. Go back.
 Judge.   I cannot shut my eyes.
 Col. Sleep open-eyed like hares, then.
 Judge.   Oh!
         [*Exit, pushed by Col.*]
 Mrs. Lamb. (*Having expressed her disgust by faces
  and gestures.*)   Beast! brute!
 Mrs. S. Oh! Sister Lamb!
 Mrs. L. (*Mockingly.*) Oh! Sister Squigginson!
(*Jeeringly.*) Child!
 Dr.   Ladies, hasten Sister Willard, please.
           [*Exeunt both.*]
(*The emphasis in proportion to Van D.'s nodding.*)
The mirage of the Savior is descried
 (*Cagliostro, gorgeously attired, rises slowly, unperceived
   by Van D. and Dr.*)

In the far cloud, by men of science.   Has
Renan not said that Science is to seize
The rudder of existence from blind Fate,
Steer from the whirlpool, — death, disease, despair, —
Where men are dashed to fragments, as were they
The glass at the marriage rite of God with Bliss?
    (Cagliostro, folding his arms, fixes his smile on Van
                      Doozer.)
  Van D. The only feasible method of reforming
The world, would be to breed up men like pacers,
Trotters, and circus leapers, as suggested
By one G. G. in a magazine.*   The state
Should not permit the ailing or poor to wed,
Nor criminal classes, —
  Dr. How prevent them, pray,
Except one with his sight could vivisect,
Not only kidneys, lungs, but hearts, souls, minds?
  Van D. By hanging them, if needs be, as old Harry
And good Queen Bess did, — and it should destroy
All weaklings at their birth.   Celibacy
And fœticide should be encouraged, dykes
Against tempestuous over population.
  Dr. (Having whistled and gestured wildly.)
Most feasible!   Good Heavens! most feasible!
Most feasible.
  Van D.   Mere sentiment, white trailing
Robe of Humanity, the infant, must
Be shortened, nay, cast off, if he would not
Grow hopelessly a womanish priest, — it must
Not trip him, bump his head, now that he walks.
  Dr. (With gusto and shutting his eyes, irritated by
                Van Doozer's nodding.)
The peacocks, in an isle, now arid grown,
Once met in furious pride to extirpate
The paler of their specie.   These were flown
At, and the sun sank, and the moon rose late,

---

* George Guilderbury must have plagiarized from Dr. T. M. Coan's Galaxy Paper on reforming the world.

Before the war was hushed, and then each pale
Lay motionless. "Hip-hip, hurray! hurray!"
The conqueror's hawked. — Ha! they began to fail,
And their eyes opened with cold, breaking day.
Dying they gurgled, "Oh! to Future's eyes
What a huge, ugly monster we shall be,
Known only by our foot-marks! our lark-rise
Of music Earth will hear no more; nor see
The sun-rise of our spread, — at which men stare,
Turning their backs on Sol, mere rising bare,
On highway! — nor behold our strut again.
Dry is our well, — the *paler* was the *hen*."

   Van D. Poor Lilla's fable prettily baby-caps
The theme, but does not helmet it for battle.

   Dr. Pray, who your trainers? Who your jockies? who
The breakers? trainers?

   Van D.   G. G. stated not.

   Dr. Perhaps the horses are to train each other?

   Van D. I answer, spirits — such as these grand peaks *
May draw to earth, — say, in a thousand years, —

   Dr. (*In Disgust.*) Some fools are distant-sighted;
what is grand
Afar off, is despicable when near;
The eagle's eye falls into that of a midge. —

   Van D. For I would be no visionary.

   Dr.   How
I pity him, Van Doozer, with an ear
For only the maddening discords! pity the owl,
Wildered mid New Year's chimes, or chimes rejoicing
With Victory, Peace! Oh! each sweet Is may not
Be, — God, or Hope, may not be — such a Savior
May not be, — Earth, sky, planets, — all may not
Be, saving within my mind. — Ha! ha!

   Van D.   May not be,†
The music of the future, grand finale.

---

  * Professor Wallace, *Fortnightly Review*, and Mr. Buckle, *History of Civilization.*   † Emanuel Swedenborg and A. J. Davis.

Dr. 'Tis easier to convince posterity
By millions, than contemporaries singly,
And this consoles me.
   Van D.   Fly to the millions, brother!
   Tempt. (*Entering.*) Egad! ha! that the engine, pa-
      tented
To lift Creation out of the eely mud?
   Ralph. (*Rushing to Tempt.*) By Jonathan, the man I
      want. I called
To-day upon you, Mr. Templeton,
To interview you. Last September, tenth,
Thirteenth, and fourteenth, and October sixth,
November sixteenth, seventeenth, generally
At ten o'clock in the evening, were you conscious
Of being present at our seance?
   Tempt.   What?
   Ralph. Did you wake up with an aching head?
   Tempt.   What do
You mean, sir?
   Van D.   That your spirit is a diner
Out.* (*Noises, and the gas-jets leap.*)
   Tempt. Precious must your nut of meaning be,
Since, like a squirrel, fountain-tailed, you hide it.
You are requested to postpone this farce
Indefinitely. Close the windows, — windy.
   Dr. Mistaken! 'tis not windy. Did you not
Drink often at my expense, sir?
   Tempt.   What?
   Ralph.   Beer, bourbon.
   Tempt. The Colonel must be drafting a regiment
Of the deranged. Beer, bourbon! — Oh! snakes! vipers!
These banished, all were Paradise; while they
   (*Cagliostro smiles at Templeton, and disappears.*)
Are extant, never an Eden.—(*To Col.*) George, your sister
Was made to swallow RUM, when physically
Unable to resist. Must she be dragged
Down? or must he be lifted up? Decide;
Which is it, Heaven or Hell?
                      * R. D. Owen.

Col.   Hell!
Ralph.   Templeton,
Do you not like long tunnels best, because,
In them, you have a chance to snatch a swig
Without eyes shining, like segars, at you?
    Mrs. L. (*re-entering.*) Go on without her; she wants
        too much coaxing.
    Tempt. Oh! to be thus calumniated drives
Me mad. Were it aught but the beastliest
Of — Oh!
    Dr.   Birds *on the wing* conceal the feet
That ran in dirty places.
    Tempt.   George, where is
Your father?
    Col.   Jaded out.
    Tempt.   Strange, — very strange!
    Col. You saw me lead him forcibly from here.
    Tempt. Reminded me of the Man in the Iron Mask.
    Col. He's old now, water-covered ice, — can bear
Scarcely the shadow of the cawing crow,
Much less the hungry talons of the osprey,
Suspense, upon its restless flight of torture.   [*Exit.*]
    Tempt. (*Following.*) Indeed! Is your poor sister
        then so strong,
She can arm off so grim a bird of prey?
Doctors how dilatory! Oh! the spirit
Of Daniel rushes through my arms.   [*Exit.*]
    Dr. (*Gazing about.*)   It don't.
    Mrs. L. Dear Lilla, here yet?
    Col. (*To Mrs. W. at door.*) Come. (*Tempt. re-enters.*)
    Mrs. W.   No; I'm no fool.
    Tempt. Indeed not.
    Mrs. W. (*To Tempt.*) It is strange, indeed, that you,
After advising me the way you did,
Should suddenly whirl about and push me on.
    Tempt. Must we act after, as before, fresh knowledge?
    Col. For Aleck's reputation make no scene.
    Tempt. Paul, after hearing the voice, "Why perse-
        cutest

Thou me?" desisted.   That thing will not bite
You, — come, dear.
   Col. Come, come. — (*Music, and the gas-jets dance.*)
   Mrs. W.   What is that?
   Tempt.   Clap-trap,
My dear.
   Mrs. W. George, why this hubbub? Are you raising
A fog for him to steal home under?   I
Am no Xantippe with a pail of water.
       (*She retreats followed by the Col.*)
Nor will I now be treated, as if one.
   Col. Come! Thought you were AFRAID to stay alone,
Though Mr. Templeton kindly volunteered
To keep you company.   Come.
   Mrs. W.   Be again
Crushed!
   Dr.   Will this lady be again crushed? (*No thumps.*)
      No!
   Mrs. S. Fear not; I do not wonder you are timid.
Oh! how I trembled ere beholding Birdie
And Birdie's papa!   Ever since, the seance
Has been a bath refreshing, nerving, gladdening.
   Tempt. One making you the cleaner in your heart?
   Van D. (*To Dr.*) Why is it preachers cannot meet
      without
Butting each other?
   Dr.   Instinct, like Cologne goats.
   Mrs. L. Ha! ha!
   Van D.   No, doctor; but because each feels
Strongly in his own head, what in the other's
He plainly sees, the horn of anti-Christ.
   Col. For Heaven's sake douse this drum ecclesiastic!
Sounds nothing but dead marches to the world.
   Mrs. S. Have you a darling gone? may be my Birdie
Will go to her and tell her you are here.
   Mrs. W. George, raise the light.
   Dr.   No; spirits cannot bear

Light, madam, any more than you can bear
A crawling, green, cold glow-worm on your eyes.
 Col. (*To Dr.*) Now open fire —
Mrs. W.   With prayer.
Col.   No.
Tempt.   Prayer by all means.
 Col. No time, no time.
 Tempt.   To pray is not to lag, sir,
But, like an elk, to kneel on highest speed
Above the land-slide, over the precipice.
 Mrs. L. (*Tired of listening.*)
Lilla says that John Keats — who, had he not
Been killed, would have been perfectest of poets —
And she are one, as Mother Lee and Christ
Are thought to be by the Shakers. See how funny
She is. She says that Shakers are Christians living
Near the much too fresh diggings of the Bible.
 Col. Hell and damnation!
 Mrs. W.   George!
 Tempt.   We should uncover,
Not only heads of hats, but minds, hearts, tongues,
Of harshness, in the presence of ladies, sir.
 Col. Damn it, we are refining so that —
 Tempt.   We!!
 Mrs. W. Offer the prayer up, Mr. Templeton.
 Tempt. With all my heart.
 Col.   Hell! Silent prayer
Is loudest, being sincerest. When one drowns,
Must we kneel, bow, or dash through the waves to him?
 Tempt. Your dashing after him would be a prayer,
A note so high that all the seraphims
Would listen for a second, then would find
It was no discord to their symphony,
The grandest of composers, from whose harp
Spring solar systems, melodizing space,
Having arranged for it ere time began,
As for true miracles, not cheats, illusions.
 Mrs. L. Pugh! will it ever begin?

Dr.   Do form the circle,
The rainbow after Superstition's deluge.
(*Around the table, which begins to swing, they sit, facing the cabinet.*)
   Mrs. W. (*Springing up.*) Lord! George! George!
   Col.   Hush! sit down — sit down.
   Mrs. S.   Mere zephyr.
   Tempt. (*To Col.*) Your plunging, like a faithful mastiff, after
The General, dragging him to the shore of duty,
Would be just such a prayer.
   Col.   By shore of duty
I know not what you mean, and will require
An explanation.
   Tempt. Very well, sir; when? (*Raps.*)
   Mrs. W. Oh!
   Tempt.   Trickery!
   Dr.   Positively no admittance
To any spirit not a philosopher. (*Increase of raps.*)
Only the highest, truest, will be welcome.
                           (*Louder raps.*)
The greatest of you all will rap, none other.
           (*Raps louder and more numerous.*)
   Tempt. No better than their brethren now on earth.
   Dr. The wisest of the Seven Old Grecian Sages
Will be the spokesman.
(*Raps are so loud, numerous, and prolonged, that the Dr. is disgusted.*)
                          I decline to help
Any more out of Charon's boat of raps,—
Most precious time! all must excuse me.
   Tempt.   Should
Make time to sieve such venerable ashes.
   Col. (*Savagely, to Dr.*) Fouracres and the General first.
   Dr.   Shall not.
One would suppose the least important thing
Here, is the Physical Savior of the Race,

To which all eyes fly, flocks from drear sea-wandering,
Deep-diving, prairie-wrecking, foresting,
Or orcharding for insect, worm, seed, fruit,
Caving, and crowding by millions — Vogel-berging —
In scientism and narrower superstition.
 Col. You circle damnably bird-like ere you perch!
 Dr. Say blessingly, as Nature in bright fruit,
Grand spheres, or God, in His eternity.
 Tempt. Father of light —
 Dr.   Hail, most illustrious friends!
Who from the past ascend and arch the earth,
As over the snow-plains, pinnacled, domed, mosqued,
Towered, castellated, mirage of the world,
Its glittering frauds, its misery, pale and prostrate, —
The streamers, merry dancers. You behold
The Savior coming in the morning clouds
Of Lilla down to men, and hence, a preface
Would be but lanterning the sunrise. Cast,
O Thou first Cause! who momently breathest millions
Of universes into love, called space,
Thy glance, like a Niagara, over us,
To cleanse us worthy of this dispensation,
This feature which alone resembles Thine,
That none may cry, like Aristotle; "I
Was born in foulness, in anxiety
Have lived, and now depart in perturbation."
 Tempt. Father of light! beneath whose wings extended
Ten million solar systems, swans with flocks,
Float ceaselessly to nestle at Thy breast,
Without whose warmth they all would perish, drift
Down dark Niagaras, be impinged to pieces, —
 Mrs. L. Heard preachers like you before — to our
  long grief. —
 Tempt. I, in the name of Thy beloved Son, ask
For these blind folk commiserating rays. (*Noises.*)
 Van D. The goose imagines God the biggest goose.
 Mrs. S. Most Christians in their lives treat Him as
  such.

Dr. (*Singing nervously.*) " Oh! how fairer than day is
 the land " --(*Stops.*)
Mrs. L., Van D., and *Mrs. S.* " Which by vision we
 soon will have here, (*Violin plays.*)
When the dearest will grasp up our hand,
Or will wipe from our eye the sad tear."
 Mrs. S. I know you by your playing, love! O Henry!
All parable is now over, over.*
 Dr.   Question
No spirit, dear; he may be garrulous, —
 Mrs. S. I knew you could not help but come to-night.—
 Dr. Delay us, be an Ancient Mariner.
                            (*A spirit appears.*)
 Mrs. S. Henry was never garrulous. —. Rebecca,
Dear, merriest daughter of our merry mother,
Old England, welcome! How bright memories flutter,
And chirp about me, flocks of English sparrows!
With you I went to hear the saintly Irving,
In his miraculous " kirk." † With you I read, —
 Dr. Oblige me, dear, by simply bowing to friends. —
 Mrs. S. Disputed with my arm around your waist, —
 Dr. You will have all eternity to talk. —
 Mrs. S. Hoped, vowed to follow Truth, eastward or
 westward,
That She should not, still further off in thickets,
Complain, " I die of thirst. No one will creep
To me with water; she may tear her train,
Or mark her arm."
 Dr.   What! my first love? — O, Mary!
Within my heart your room is as you left it,
No object sacrilegiously eloined, —
Thrown out; no book, chair, flower displaced. I sit
Within it oft, expecting you will enter,
Your virtue-slippered feet reverberating
So plainly that you seem not yet departed,
But hastily returning, open-armed,
For one more kiss, embrace.

      * Lady Hester Stanhope.
      † See *Life of Edward Irving*, by Mrs. Oliphant.

    Mrs. L.　　　　　　　　　Pugh! you? begone!
Big porpoise! that, upon the *finest* day,
Would fetch a storm along wherever you rolled!
Sneak! that in the day would bend to lift no stone,
But in the night, when I lay fast asleep,
Would break my windows in, smash in my skull,
Uncover me and Lilla to dire draughts!
    Dr. Pythagoras, most welcome! I admire
The five years' silence of your neophytes; —
'Twas a high mountain source of a broadening river —
    Mrs. L. Yet, never did I in my drunkardness —
    Dr. Of wisdom. — Will not sister Lamb restrain? —
    Mrs. L. While my poor post of a husband held a horse,
Or sponged a mule, or wagon, for a drink, —
Smother a child in bed, or let one tumble
Into a tub and drown, as you did, after
Returning home from church, where, in the hymning,
You and your old hag mother had been steepling
On either side of that black-whiskered villain.
    Tempt. Is not the atmosphere here most miasmal?
    Dr. Uncharitable thoughts, retaliations,
Are tools of the Stone Age, sister Lamb, which Christians
Use with a savage's dexterity,
But which hands, softened with enlightenment, never
Should touch.
    Col.　　　　Touch bottom and rebound soon, or —
    Dr. Meet is it, love, you come to share my glory.
    Mrs. L. How dare you come to see my Lilla crowned?
You'd rather see her gibbeted.
    Tempt.　　　　　　　　　　　　We leave
This tunnel, Black-hole; Colonel, lead.
    Mrs. W.　　　　　　　　　　　　　Yes.
    Col.　　　　　　　　　　　　　　Nervous?
    Tempt. Of what? Pshaw! not a particle.
    Mrs. L. (*The spirit retreating, having by posture and
        gesture purposely irritated her.*) You better
Go, you old barren slattern! —
    Mrs. S.　　　　　　　　　　　　Sist —

Mrs. L. That used
To break a character and heart, like eggs,
Into your tea at every meal, to make
It tasty, as with milk from clover meadow.
   Dr. Quiet, dear sister, till the Savior's birth,
The rainbow has been rounded on the earth.
   Mrs. L. How dare she come here? I would cut my
      throat
To get at her. How happy but for her!
Between the stitches of her hymn and prayer, —
Ha! making dresses for the brighter world,
Without once mending the tatters that she wore, —
She told me how that devil wanted me
At the camp-meeting, — *soul-trap!*
         (*The spirit appears as a girl.*)
   Mrs. S. Birdie! Birdie!
O fairest, brightest blossom of my love!
   Mrs. L. You nasty, gaby, snuffy brat, that came
In where you had no right to come!
   Tempt. Oh! shame!
The heat of Satan here is most oppressive.
   Mrs. S. Decking yourself with seaweeds like a crab,
The little mimicking brother of the world,
You darling? Kiss me, lay your cheek on mine.
Did papa not come too?
   Spirit. (*In torn dress and seaweed.*) O mamma! mam-
      ma!
Does mamma not know Emma, who was drowned?
Whose grave is morning-gloried? that she did
Not kiss good-by to?
   Mrs. W. What! my God! my child, —
My Emma?
   Spirit. Your own Emma, now an angel.
   Mrs. W. Oh! I must clasp my darling.
   Col. Jane, be cautious.
   Spirit. No, mamma; it would make me melt from you,
And never might you see me any more.
Sad was I when the Savior, kissing me,
Hid you from sight, though only a moment.

Mrs. W.   Oh!
Were papa and mamma not, my darling Emma,
The first-born of your loving lips? first angel
That broke through the bright, divine and everlasting
Impression of the Savior's mouth on yours?
   Spirit. Yes, mamma, that he might lift you up, too,
Though I thought you too heavy for his knee;
He smiled and said, I might go down to you;
And soon I saw with pain that you loved me
Too madly, mamma. Oh! in the lilac lane
You found a girl, and in your heart declared
She had no mamma, else she were not lost,
Though was I not myself once lost in the woods,
When after morning-glories?
   Mrs. W.   Oh!
   Spirit.   Fool's errand!
For, like good children, they stay round the house,
As you told me when putting me to bed
Without my supper, —
   Mrs. W.   Oh! —
   Spirit.   Though you let slip
A cake and peach, when you thought me not looking.
   Mrs. W. Did my own darling see me in the lane?
   Spirit. You grabbed her in your arms, extinguishing
Her kicking, screaming, with caresses, kisses,
And shouted, "My own Emma!" —
   Mrs. W.   Emma, my love!
   Spirit. And felt like running off you knew not where
       to, —
O mamma! mamma! God was looking down,
Like a hot sun, upon you, till that moment,
When, clouding his face, he turned away *forever* —
   Mrs. W. My God! —
   Spirit. It seemed. Thick, choking darkness gathered
Then all about me, —
   Mrs. W.   Why did you not speak? —
   Spirit. Till up the sun whirled, like a fire tornado,
When you recalled Lord Jesus' half-crazed mother
Upon the three days' search.

Mrs. W. Oh! I must clasp
My darling angel, Emma, to my heart,
Must never let her go.
Tempt. Step cautiously;
When in the dark, you must expect a downfall
Through scratching briars. or into snake-holes, bear-traps,
May get your head lopped off.
Col. (*Bitterly at his own powerlessness.*) Ha!
Tempt. Ha-ing at *me*,
Sir?
Mrs. W. Emma, one kiss! Oh, one caress!
Spirit. No, mamma,
I cannot till, by a second ceremony,
You heal dear papa, whose poor head you gashed
Red open with your actions, for he thought
You knew of the flaw, were baffling it from mind.
Mrs. W. My God! what flaw?
Tempt. What flaw?
Col. (*Puzzled.*) No flaw! Dam'd strange!
Mrs. W. Did you and father not make sure of the law?
Col. Assuredly, and did our best to make
Him think so, but,—
Mrs. W. But what?
Col. It preyed on his mind.
Mrs. W. What?
Col. That, as the judge who granted his divorce
Became insane, the judgment may be questioned,
Reversed.
Mrs. W. Oh!
Spirit. This is why dear papa took
To drink, though on the secret.
Tempt. Ha!
Spirit. " Forgive him,
Ma. Pitying, lift him up. Faith is the walking
On tip-toe through this slushy world."
Tempt. What!

Spirit.   Some
" May dance ascetically on their toes,
But, tiring out soon, they splash down like swine.
Ah! very few can keep on tiptoe long;
The best will slip, nay, slide," — like boys on ice,
For the delight of tumbling oftenest.
    Mrs. W. Oh!
    Tempt. Now or never, save her, — come, my child.
    Col. Here, no bulldozing, Luther ended that.
God! I would end this if I could, — *I will.*
    Spirit. Profanity makes me melt — Oh! (*Retreats.*)
    Mrs. W.   Emma!
    Van D. (*To Col.*) Silence! Or I will be the pitchfork, you the hay.
    Mrs. W. Wait! Emma! Emma!
    Spirit.   Oh! your calling pains
Me, mamma. Do not — though it terribly aches
Me saying so — call me again till after
The re-adjusting rite, the rocket to rise
And peak or crater the earth with stars as soon
As lighted by the incandescent presence
Of your poor sister, at whose throbbing throat
A bowie, like the teeth of a springing panther,
Is glistening. It was cruel, —
    Mrs. W.   Sister!
    Spirit.   In*deed*,
Who would have pushed you from the ghastliest chasm
Back into an abyss not near so ghastly,
And who will prove herself more sisterly still.
    Mrs. W. Oh!
    Tempt. Colonel!
    Col. Then help Jane by adding a brace —
Since it is Willard's whim — upon the marriage.
    Dr. He need not, for a bishop has volunteered.
    Mrs. W. Wait! wait! I have a thousand things to ask, —
Where is your papa? Am I being deceived?
My dear will tell no lie.

Spirit.   Oh! agony,
To break my clasping arms of sight from you,
My own dear mamma! But I must, I must.
A spirit flings the bowie, like a fire-fly,
From your sad sister, and conducts her hither,
While clouds, the weeping saviors of the world,
Rise all transfigured to the meteor-fall,
Which Papa rides down from Vermilion Mars,
Like Putnam down the steps, or like himself —
   Mrs. W. Emma! O Emma! will you leave me? Oh!
   Mrs. S. She will come back soon. I know how you
      feel.
   Dr. Madam, this marriage question, which has vexed
The sages of all ages, will be settled
Soon to the satisfaction of both sides.
How simple are the ways of God *when known!*
With the few fingers of His elements,
What a magician, not alone with seasons
And clouds, but with the hearts and minds of men!
   Tempt. If you can stand this longer, Colonel, —
   Mrs. W.   Oh!
The morning-glories, pears, and grapes, and cake —
   Tempt. You have a stomach — aye, the bulimia —
For folly, I must say.
   Mrs. W.   The lane, — my darling!
   Mrs. S. (*To a male spirit appearing.*)
Henry! dear Henry!
   Dr. Hail, Pythagoras!
   Spirit. There is a disturbing influence.
   Mrs. L.   Put him out.
   Spirit. 'Tis Sister Lamb.
   Mrs. L.   What!
   Spirit.   Till she goes the General
Cannot appear.
   Col. Then out with her, — this way, ma'am.
   Mrs. L. How dare you pluck me, you old warm-
      nosed pup!
   Van D. Lay not a finger on this lady, —

Col.   Hell!
Van D. Who will comply with the spirit's wishes.
Mrs. L.   Never!
You bowsprit-nosed, red, pimpled-faced, cow-jawed,
Cat-footed sneak! would you have me pitched out
From being present at my grandchild's birth,
When I am to have my eyes opened? not
That mine were bunged by flying wood — ha! ha!
A flying fist. "Poor thing!" say all the neighbors,
She will not bleed to death for want of cobwebs."
There would have been no good just God in Heaven
Had you escaped without a broken neck.
    Dr. Why is it, spirit, Sister Lamb should leave?
    Mrs. L. Sha'n't. Lilla would not let me stay with her,
But promised, if I came — I use her words, —
To dress me up "in trailing silks of glory,
Like those proud autumn rustles in from sea
To sea, tempest to calm, the Sun, train-bearer,
That I shall need a comet space in turning."
Off! Would I go in Heaven if you were there?
Before all angels I would draw my skirts
Up to my knees from touching you, you dirt,
Slush, puddle! —
    Dr. Tool of the Stone Age, dear. —
    Female Spirit. (*Appearing.*)   We angels
Have no desire to see your skeletons.
    Tempt. Shocking! —
    Mrs. L.   As you once did to me on the street, —
Mean when you closed your clams of eyes at me
And tumbled — Oh! I felt so glad — right into
The water trough, and where I — ha! ha! — would
Have let you drown, had I not gotten a glimpse
Of my lost balmoral. — An angel? *devil!* —
Lilla, are you not here yet?
    Dr.   In due time, dear.
    Mrs. W. My darling, if you are now here, do speak.
    Col. Hem!
    Tempt.   I will brace the marriage, end the farce.

Male Spirit. Will Sister Lamb not go?
Mrs. L. No, never!
Col. Must.
Female Spirit. The preacher must go, too; should take her arm.
Male Spirit. Let him remain, for does he not resemble
A great apostle?
Female Spirit. Verily the one
Who died of a sore throat; for in each woman
He spies his Lord, and kisses to betray.
   Tempt. (*Flinging a rope at the female spirit, and clutching the male, whom she pushes in his way.*)
Human or devil! I will strangle you.
Victory!
Mrs. W. George! George!
Col. Come quickly. (*Exit with Mrs. W.*)
Mrs. S. What is it?
Mrs. L. A spirit is pushing the coarse disturber out.
Male Spirit. Oh! Oh! Your eyes are burning glasses, grape-shot! *
Direct their deadly fire elsewhere — *on him.*
Have spirits, when in human form, no feeling?
   (*Dr. jerks Tempt. aside, thereby releasing the spirit, who disappears.*)
Tempt. As I conjectured, they are vulnerable
As Africans upon the shin-bone. That
One should have been more expeditious crossing
The fence between both worlds, not let me catch
His tissue paper trowsers, like a bull-dog. (*Flourishes his trophy,*)
Mrs. L. You brought that tissue paper in your pocket.
Tempt. Let us thank God for the capture of the shark,
And be not fools, dear friends, to bathe again
In these dark waters.
Dr. Sister Lamb and brother

---

* Andrew Jackson Davis, *The Diakka.*

Van Doozer, go for Lilla, since she is
Unable to project her spirit hither.
  Ralph. (*Re-entering.*) Be not deceived by the pretended capture
And suffering of a harlequin Diakka.
  Dr. The rope from Heaven is whizzing through my hands, —
Help me to make earth fast. Too many ages
Has she been foot-ball to most furious billows.
  Mrs. L. Lilla is dead, else she would now be here.
                                                       [*Exit.*]
  Van D. What ever you desire will be performed
With pleasure. You shall never say that I
Let damp upon your powder; though, if I
Were you, I would not be too confident
That it will blast earth, snowy mountainous
With evil, into scarlet rolling prairies,
But be well satisfied if I could bring
Willard and family over to the cause.
  Ralph. Yes, thousands would follow; it would be the rage.
  Dr. How I thank God that I am neither of you!
Oh! were she here! (*Exeunt Van D. and Ralph.*)
  Patsy. (*Entering, having struck ten times on his bottle.*)   Tin sharp. I come to bury
The Gineral in the consacrated ground
Of matrimony, that his sowl may rest
In pace. Where is the couple to be hand-cuffed?
Like smiling pris'ners, going to the Tombs,
With paler on the left, and politician
With pin-wheel of a tongue upon the right,
And a kite's tail of boys and girls a-following.
  Cag. (*With low sweet voice describing the mirage seen through the walls.*)
Into the stream at a crab, which decorates
Itself with medals and epaulets of straws,
The crouching ape peeps over, imitates,

And, tickled at his reflection, claps his paws
Into fine hands, stretches erect, and then
Laughs heartily into the beautiful First of men.
    Dr. Peace, spirits, peace! I will not lend an ear
To any other discord! harsh disturbance.
    Patsy. How hungry Moses' teeth-marks shine! rich
        ear-ring!
    Cag. At him, dark spirits, wild beasts, birds of prey,
Nature, Society, and Superstition,
Under dark, clashing clouds, dash, swoop, essay
To rend him piece-meal ere the high position
Of sheltered peace is his. He does not fall,
But, with new strength developed, conquers all.
    Dr. Dear Lilla *has* projected her spirit hither.
    Cag. On lightning, Borak, winged horse of the skies,
He leaps, dashes at distance, hughest sea,
Prairie, and mountain monster, and this lies
Down in its blood, is buried instantly
With mammoth and sea-serpent by land-slide
Of towns with temples, schools, both purified.
    Dr. Aye, verily! If I had not destroyed
That monster, I might still have doubted, caviled
That man's amelioration is too near.
    Patsy. I'll wait no longer, I'm insoolted. Phew!
(*Tosses the redeemer, and, as he disappears, beckons to comrades outside to blow and rattle. Templeton endeavors to escape, but is frightened back by the tin-pans and fish-horns.*)
    Dr. God! all is lost, lost!
    Cag. (*Unseen and with a deep, sorrowful voice to Templeton.*)   Saul! why persecutest
Thou me? Snuff thou the candle bright that ages
May whirl about it, like moth swarms of spheres.
Lovest thou me so little that thou fearest
The smarting of thy finger-tips?
    Tempt.   My God! —
But blasphemy! blasphemy! if men say, "Lo! Christ

Is in the desert, closet, know them liars."
"Not though an angel, dewy with heaven," says Paul.
[*Hastens out.*]
   Dr. Can it be Man is a Sisyphus, condemned
To roll a rocky god up to the summit
That it may then crash down upon his head?
What can I, crushed and bleeding, answer?
   Mrs. S.   Welcome
Good Lord! hail! welcome! On my donkey, too,*
As white as driven snow, which Beauty canters
On over the prairie. How unworthy the world!
We all, good Lord! "Oh! would I were a tropical
Summer to scatter flowers before Thee slowly,
And, throated with a million birds, seas, forests,
With angels sing:

> Hail, thou most Holy One!
>   Whose listening is like air
> To each sad, lowly one,
>   Healing and every where!

Like freshening air, — Oh! mountain air
Which reddens the cheek from pale despair,
Or ocean air, which broadens the chest
Like wide-winged billows, frightened from nest."
Good Lord, I have sung alto, used the words
Of Lilla, just that she might sing soprano,
Attract thy glance, and, like May's flowery tide,
Rise at thy bidding.
   Dr.   I would not deprive
A star-fish of one ray, though it develop
A large, swift radiant, as the brilliant scatterings
Of Sol in his primeval whirl grew Suns,
Lest in the parent I inflict a pang, — (*views the mirage.*)
O, black-winged, blasphemous, thought avaunt! avaunt!
Thou shalt not beat my head in with thy wing,
Nor break my arm, and drag me to thy eyrie

---

* Lady Hester Stanhope.

To glut thy clamorous, harpy brood, despairs. —
What! my own Father could, with cheats, illusions,
Pull me apart? a fangless, milk-white moth,
Who strikes unvelvetly against no creature,
And fain would lead quintillions over sea,
Marsh, desert, into fragrant Summerland.
    Cag. (*Disappearing.*)
Touched by his hand, each spirit and wild bird
Whitens, grows tame. How gorgeous, sportive, free,
Amid sun-showers! They scatter. What yet heard
Was such ear-rapture! Roaring monopoly
He slaughters, gives all men a barbecue.
There! down the Scarlet Woman drops, gored through.
    Mrs. S. Lord! is Thy coming only a passing breeze,
Which lets our feverish heads blaze up again?

ACT. V.

(*The gas-jets, being at the point of flaring, dance responsive to the low music of the spirits, and when they burn low, the rooms are faintly illuminated by the forest fire. Ralph Raymond and Van Doozer have just carried Lilla Lamb on a litter toward the redeemer, which has been mended.*)

    Van D. The rattle-snake is in her throat. Poor Psyche!
    Dr. Brother, you talk like one who has the horrors.
    Van D. Faith, that cures others, may cure her.—Consumption,
A bouquet-maker, picks our loveliest flowers.
    Dr. A telegram! a glorious telegram!—
    Ralph. A message, hear.—(*Rushes toward Dr.*)
    Dr. "All, spirit or human, horned
With fossilized ideas, infuriate
To bully, roar me down, will have their horns
Eradicated, like a vicious tooth,
To their delight; for otherwise, blood, ruin,
Instead of progress, joy, the blue sea, drifted

By un-Promethean false religion, hugest
Black water-spout, till long white streaks of clouds,
Would drown the cries of anguish, deluge the earth."
    Ralph. Peace! glory! Oh, for words to utter our
        joy!
On, Brother! on, on, on! on, on, on, on!
This message sent to you is signed by Plato,
Pythagoras, Empedocles, Confucius,
Morgan the Buccaneer, and Cagliostro,
Mormon Joe Smith, Tom Paine, and John of Leyden, —
There, such a long list, you must look it down.
    (*Lifts the scroll which unrolls to his feet.*)
    Dr. Van Doozer, how is that? you said that spirits
Of the first magnitude keep coldly afar
From earth, —
    Van. D. Or dwindle into a pinch of starch,
Fall into hysterics. Brother Squigginson,
If un-Promethean false religion be
The water-spout, you draw it down again
By your theistic notions.
    Dr.   Be not led
By your enormous nose — a forty footer —
    (*Van D. measures his nose with his finger and shows
        the Dr. the result.*)
Of predeliction, Brother Smith Van Doozer.
    Van D. (*Pleasantly.*) My golden rule is, Brother
        Squigginson,
Never to reason —
    Dr.   So I always thought. —
    Van D. Never to reason with one when the dust
Of anger reddens his fast-blinking eyes. —
I wish dark cabinets were abolished.
    Ralph.   Do you?
Because the press would cry them down? what is
The press itself but a dark cabinet? how
I laugh at the gullibility of thousands,
Who, daily, swallow stenching stuff for manna
Handed down by God!

Van D. I dread dyspepsia, —
Ralph. Is history not, at each grand epoch, molded
By hidden hands, as nature from the marble
Of Winter into the living group of Spring?
Dark cabinets are the vestibules of progress.
  Van D. (*With provoking slowness.*)
And, therefore, am no hasty swallower, Ralph.
  Dr. (*Contemptuously to Van D.*) Thick are your
    pearls of ocular delusion,
When you think such a fire tornado, darkness. (*Points
    to Lilla.*)
  Van D. (*Whispering.*) How?
  Dr. How is the reign of the Upper Powers, — enough
For us to have the glorious ride.
  Van D.   Ha!
  Dr.   Go,
Go, I feel awkward, stupid, overshadowed
By such a superior, hawk that swoops and circles
About me, fancying he smells my doom.
  Van D. Were all my wishes realized, would I
Be happier? I would want more worlds to conquer;
Why then suppose all others would have peace,
Were all their aspirations crowned, tiaraed?
  Dr. Go, — why here anyhow?
  Van D. (*Smiling.*) The snow, light, has
To fall. What! fear my presence is a whirlwind
Against it? can it be blown off to sea?
  Dr. I loathe the chameleonic-headed, hearted,
People who crawl along half dead. Show me
A man who can erupt his own opinions,
Though they may cloud, or crimson, all creation,
And I respect him; but a thing that crawls,
Reflecting other men's mud mountains — Oh!
Go, let us part in friendship ere too late. (*Offers his
    hand, but turns away disgusted, Van D. respond-
    ing with only a finger.*)
  Van D. Only for me would you have Lilla here?
I, who have opened my veins that she might drink

And strengthen, and again would open them,
And with this hand have slaughtered the leaping elk,
And bison lowering at me like a storm,
Require no passport, Squigginson, to be
Here when the last resort, great gun, is fired
To raise her sunken body to the surface.
   Dr. Great gun indeed! It will raise up the world,
Who has gone down a third time, first as Pagan,
Second as Papist, third as Protestant.
   Van D. (*Pleasantly.*) The last, worst, horriblest calamity
Which could befall man, Brother Squigginson,
Would be his grasping of *all truth.** (*Noises outside.*)
   Dr. (*Hastening to door.*)   Ha! ha!
   Van. D. (*Following a few steps.*)
I say this to console you.
   Lilla. (*In a trance.*)   Ha! aha!
" My heart aches, and a drowsy numbness pains
My sense, as though of hemlock I had drunk,
Or emptied some dull opiate to the drains
One minute past, and Lethe-wards had sunk;—"
O pain, away! away, with face distort,
With fingers bloody with thick clots of hair,
With staggering gait on this firm earth! False love,
Thou serpent-fanged with everlasting night,
Away! Away, huge, rabid Might that snappest
At weaker-winged, but far more beautiful, Right!
The fittest to survive is the beautiful.
Off, all ye Furies! go and gulp dark hemlock,
Mankind are in the Fane forevermore,
Aye, in the ark with *every* beautiful thing.
   Van D. (*Musingly.*) Thy fire of Faith, my poor, dear child, must not
Wane ashen-low, if it would burn disease
Out, but must rage, and, therefore, must I pile
Faggot on faggot. Dearest, sweetest one,
Little dost thou suspect how passionately

          * Sir W. Hamilton.

This old fool loves thee. Thou art heart and head
Over all women he has ever met;
Beside thee all seem dwarfs, who might swing under
The Chinese oak, which grows full in a flower-pot,
Or might be deluged with one wind-blown dew.
  (*Kisses her impulsively.*)
 Lilla. Dear Keats, sweet Cupid, haste to Psyche. She
Will scream not, if the hot oil of thy glances
Fall on her; nor, like a decoy-duck frighted
Into its primitive nature, fly to the clouds;
But will dream on, dream brighter dreams than ever.
Her love for thee surpasses thine for her.
Oh, for a life-long kiss! Oh, for the heaven-flash
That dies not on true, loving lips, but lights
Our hearts, souls, lives, forever, like a sun!
Wert thou to sail to Ceres, pale red star,
Nor think of earth but as a rock, sand-bar,
Or iceberg, which thy happy bark once grated
Against, nor think at all of her translated
By thee to Heaven,—not that I foolishly think
That thou, Keats, couldst, each life-drop being a link,—
Oh! chain me like a felon down to earth
By arrowing me with absence! no, no, no!—
Still, on thy memory, would I linger bright,
As Sol will ever on, " Let there be Light."
 Col. (*Rushing toward Dr., then intercepting Mrs.
  Lamb.*)
This is no hospital,—by the eternal—
You shall not enter.
 Mrs. L.   You old brute! I shall.
 Col. Out!
 Mrs. L. I shall enter in spite of you. Get out
Yourself, you need an airing worse than I do.—
 Dr. As you were a disturbing influence
Before, dear Sister Lamb, do me the favor—
 Mrs. L. (*Striving hard to enter.*) You smell so of the
  drug-shop and the grave.—
 Dr. Of staying out now.

Col. (*Aiming a pistol at the Dr.'s head.*) Clear them
    out this instant,
Or I shall blow your brains out.
    Mrs. S. (*Entering.*) Oh! will not
Some spirit please disarm him?
    Van D. (*Disarming and throwing the Col.*) There
    shall not
Be a disturbing influence this time.
Hand me a rope.
    Col. (*Struggling.*) Hell! Thunder and lightning!
    murder!
    Dr. There. (*Hands a rope, and with it Van D. fas-
    tens the Col.'s arms and legs.*)
Sonny, spare your lungs, we will not lynch you.
I pitch you on the train from off the track.
    Lilla. (*Coughing.*) Ha, ha, aha! — ha, ha! — Oh!
    Mother, —
    Mrs. L.   What, dear?
    Lilla. Come nearer, for it pains me to speak loud.
    Van D. All Future is her Raphael, he will halo
Her head with stars.
    Ralph.   Clouds, pouring, formed a canon
Above Empedocles, I saw them.
    Dr. (*Straightening.*)   Did you?
    Ralph. Northward they mingled into a water-spout,
Black bodied, crested and winged with lambent sunlight,
An eagle that would lightning-claw earth heavenward!
    Van D. Speak lower, sweet Psyche sleeps; — there,
    she is wakening.
    Dr. Exactly, Ralph! What two see is objective,
Certain.
    Lilla. (*Having listened.*) Aha! ha! (*Cheerily*).
    I am after falling
Upon a bed of stiff, brown leaves. I thought
Autumn, with harshest voice, which made tall trees,
Proud Niobes, bow low with sorrow, — for
It dashed their hundred children from their arms
And scattered them from reach, — spake thus: " Believe

No promise, seed, for it must rot ere flowering;
And thou must come and be my Proserpine."
My dreams prove contrary.
    Mrs. L.   Always, always!
    Lilla.   I
Am happy as the lark that echoes Heaven,
Like a green gap with cliffs innumerable.
    Van D. (*To Ralph, entering.*)
The first, bright dogma of her faith has ever
Been, there is no true lover but the poet.
    Lilla. (*Smiling.*) I would not have a half moon, nor
        a crescent,
Which satisfies the prosy, or half-owl.
I knew poetic justice — not that merely
Of Drama, or Romance, — the long expected
Of nations, would descend, at last; nor, like
The lightning, take a flying peep at men.
The feeling that I was the most important
On earth was not conceit, but consciousness
Of my true dignity, the abdicating
Of which would have been cringing to spiders, mice,
Been treason to myself and all mankind, —
Oh! rankest blasphemy to my Creator.
I always felt as a half or bound Prometheus,
And so did Keats; both longed to seize the fire
For cold, dark earth. Ha! ha!
    Mrs. L.   Do rest, my dear.
    Mrs. S. Her thoughts are wandering, like the breaking
        clouds
After the Sun is set. — You will arise, Love!
    Dr. (*Kissing Lilla.*) You word it most delightfully,
        sweet Psyche!
    Lilla. Oh! — I'm not tired now, I could run around
The cornfield, swollen-cheeked with milk or cider,
As in the game of jocund hallow-eve. (*Rises and falls.*)
Oh! bring me to the window, for I long
To hug the mountains with my spirit arms,
As balconied Juliet, her Romeo.

Dr. The smoke of the forest fire doors up the mountains
To-night, dear.
    Lilla.   Oh! menagerie-tents then. Fancy
The poor birds, beasts, in huddling, screaming flight;
Thus, millions, with their features lightning-splashed,
Seek shelter from the darkening dust, want, woe,
The shaggy hounds that seize men by the throats.
What joy to be their shelter!
    Ralph. (*Hypnotizing Lilla with a bright metalic ball.*)   She needs rest,
Should now reserve some vigor for the crisis.
    Mrs. W. (*Entering followed by Tempt.*)
My Emma's presence proves the seance heavenly.
    Mrs. S. Angels bring us the object of our wishes
Ere these can speak, stretch out their arms, can more
Than fix their wondering, infant gaze on it.
    Mrs. W. (*To Tempt.*)   Did you not urge me to the seance to-night?
    Tempt. I thought it shallow, fordable without
The dampening of our feet, not having sunken
Yet to our waists in mud; if we attempt
Another crossing, it may cost our lives.
    Van D. Another?
    Dr. (*Approaching Tempt.*)   *No, siree!* don't honor us
With your attendance, save your hands and feet
Are fastened together.
    Tempt.   Like a sheep for slaughter?
    Dr. You brought the rope here. *I* have oft submitted
To such a test.
    Tempt.   *I thought* that I could lasso
A ghost.
    Van D.   You are a disturbing influence;
Go.
    Mrs. W. Shall go, too, then.
    Tempt.   Come, my dear.
    Col.   Stay, stay.

Mrs. W. Where are you, George?
Col. Here.
Mrs. W. Where?
Tempt. What! playing hide
And seek? — Is not this whole affair, dear child,
As I suggested, a saturnalian freak?
   Col. (*To Dr.*) Dispense with your damn'd shackling.
   Dr. I shall not.
What! at the coming of each kindly spirit
Must I exclaim, "Hands off!" to this real savage,
Who has to maul the strangers, the white faces?
   Tempt. I cannot, as your pastor — and *I will* not —
Let you be ruined, — *that was not Emma.*
   Mrs. S. How
Do you know?
   Mrs. W. Peace, peace, Mister Templeton,
Disturb my soul no more. Oh! why did I,
At first, not see my actions were the axe,
Which split poor Aleck's head red open? Why,
Like the brute soldier, did I drive a spear,
A foul thought, into his poor side? O Aleck!
Aleck!
   Tempt. Come, be not of the bright elect,
Deceived by signs and lying wonders. Come.
   Mrs. S. Your child and gallant husband may be at
Each shoulder to transport you, like bright wings.
   Mrs. W. Oh! I will go, — which is the way? the way?
Oh, for one glimpse of them! but one embrace!
One pressure to fill up this vacant heart!
   Tempt. Here, all alone! — where are your father,
      brother?
   Col. Here.
   Tempt. Fluttering, like a goose with head off.
   Col. Hell!
   Tempt. Come. I know well the demon I caught was
      flesh, —
   Dr. Must my Familiar now convince you gently,
As he convinced the Colonel in the tent? — (*Col. stirs.*)

Tempt. But with him came The Liar, —
Van D. (*Having found something with which to fasten Tempt.*) Eureka ! —
Tempt. Murderer
From the beginning, — hungry, thunderous lion
That, hundred-headed, shadows generations
Of scattering mortals, snaps their heads off, — (*Noises.*)
Dr. Fudge!
I, the director here, will brook no jargon. —
Tempt. Arms, bodies, — boyhood, girlhood, prime, age, whole
Existences with their immortal souls.
Van D. (*About to seize Tempt.*) Is that the reason of your headlessness?
Mrs. L. Alfred! (*Embraces Tempt.*)
Tempt. Lord! who are you?
Mrs. L. Oh! Heaven on earth
This day, indeed! as Lilla predicted. Come, (*Pulls him toward Lilla.*)
Come, we will cling to you forever. Oh!
My tear-blind eyes are opened, indeed.
Tempt. (*Trying to extricate.*) Let go, —
She is insane, poor thing!
Mrs. L. Upon your preaching
About the hungry, loud, soul-snapping lion,
A streak of lightning split through the black past
Zigzagly till it lighted up your face,
(*Whispering.*) As on the night you ivied, as you said,
Your arms eternally around my neck,
And swore on the Bible that you loved but me.
Oh! memory, twice or thrice this evening, sparkled
Across your features, like a firefly, but
Flashed elsewhere ere I got a second glance.
Tempt. I know you not.
(*Tries harder to extricate himself.*)
Mrs. L. So Peter said of Christ.
I would have rushed up to the pulpit twice,
Your sermon stirred me so, but that I fainted,

And would have followed you, but that I did
Not want to make you wretched, like myself.
    Tempt. Black-mail! conspiracy!
    Mrs. L.   All I forgive —
    Dr. Dark deeds may run from sight, but they return
On us with hydrophobiac teeth.
    Mrs. L.   All, Alfred, —
The tearing of my children, flesh and blood,
From me by my exasperated husband,
Your cold neglect, the torture of long years,
Mouth-twisting whisper, nudging, fingering scorn,
And lifting of white skirts from me like dirt, —
Oh! shuddering from me, as from lidless coffin
Floated out of its grave of years by the rain —
Now that I have you in my arms once more.
    Tempt. Her daughter a Madonna, — *pitiable!*
    Dr. By reparation beat the hound off, brain him.
Why skulk or scamper with him at your heels?
Nor be, as thousands are, held still at bay.
    Mrs. L. (*Dragging Tempt.*) Come, kiss her! kiss her!
— seventeen times for birth-days.
You need not let her now know why.
    Tempt. (*Breaking away then caught by Van D.*) Crazed!
       crazed!
    Mrs. W. These uninvited people will please leave.
    Dr. Brother, shake moral-suasion's hand, wait not
Till, rat-like, smoked out with the light excessive
Of the redeemer. Wed her willingly,
Before your horn has been wrenched off perforce.
    Van D. Have you the ring?
    Tempt.   This haggard fury!
    Mrs. L.   What!
    Dr. You are well paired, as even your Lilla's eyes,
Which, from their sunny dove-flight in blue skies,
Have rarely lowered, but flown right on, Man being
Their Venus, earth the car.
    Mrs. L.   One kiss at least, —

Lilla. (*Wakening.*) Get something, mother, I am
    hungry now.
Mrs. L. Yes, darling, I have brought the chicken
    broth. (*Looks for it.*)
Lilla. If you cared much for me, you would not leave
    me.
Sick people soon see that they are not wanted.
People don't like you always in their houses,
They told me to my face so. Oh! how cold
My feet are! Warm a smoothing-iron, please.
    Tempt. Shall I release you, Colonel?
    Van D.   Try it.
    Col.   No.
    Mrs. W. Emma, my angel! if you be now here,
Direct me; be not mute as in the lane.
    Tempt. Jane! Come with me, poor child! come
    from this choke-damp
To fresh, bright air. My arm.
    Mrs. W.   No.
    Tempt.   *You will not?* [*Exit.*]
    Mrs. L. Gone?
    Dr. Sister, the redeemer will soon heal
All cravings of the heart, wide, bleeding gashes.
    Mrs. L. Without one kiss! Oh! we shall follow him.
    Lilla. A kiss for whom, ma?
    Mrs. L.   You, my love.
    Lilla.   For me?
I am not dying.
    Mrs. L. No, indeed, dear,— have
The broth now? It is cold, though.
    Lilla.   I am full.
    Dr. Whether man rose from slime, or grew from ape,
Thou didst bend over, Sire! didst warmly breathe
Through his pale lips the reddening breath of mind,
Bequeathing him a hunger to behold Thee,
An upward impulse that can loiter not,—
    Lilla. I wish this dress were finished. I doubt
    much—

Dr. For it burns fiercelier than dread Fire, the wildest
Of red inhabitants of forest, prairie.—
Lilla. If girls will follow me in this reform ; —
Dr. With reason, memory of Thee, compares
He all those challenging, like Liberalism,
Science, and Christianism, "Go thou no further ; " —
Lilla. They are so fond of being squeezed to death. —
Dr. But minds them not; for each, though it horizon
The earth aurorally,— ah! sensibly,
Not rationally, — is too prone to narrow
A jerking noose around opponents' throats,
And narrowing is no lineament of Thine ;
Hence, up he struggles with hunger still more maddening.
Lilla. Would time, that crawls on caterpillar legs,
Were golden-winged ! Oh, I am icy cold
With thy delay, dear Keats ! Didst thou not say
We were one creature, each a heavenly wing,
And, separated, each a lifeless thing ?
That with stupendous marvels from all regions,
Strange languages, prophetic visions, cures,
We builded such a spacious nest that none,
Glancing at it, could think of limiting
Our range, or of prescribing that which we
Could catch, bring earthward ?
Mrs. S. Patience, Lilla, dear.
Lilla. Oh ! for the day when all are poets, not
Alone in insight, grasp, but action ! when
We need not lasso thoughts, or tame them down
And hold them, like a hostler, for the straddling
Of lazy Stupor, who sees only the dust,
Raised by them in their galloping to heaven,
And is ere long unhorsed ! when we may leap
From steed to steed of the upward-rushing millions,
As lightnings leap from cloud-caved wave to wave !
Dr. No matter where we turn, our sight is lidded
Down by machinery, fuming swallower
Of stream and forest. Young men in their strength,

And maidens in their beauty, by the millions,
It crushes with its alligator teeth
From the glad sun — his rise, warm, flowery spring,
With gay, bright songsters, streaming from the blackness
Of winter foraging, or natal grove,
As the aurora in the spectral iceland;
His noon, fruit-fulgent summer; and his set,
Prognosticative of a fairer morrow,
The gorgeous, Protean, foliage-clouded autumn.
What! such a thing a development of Thine?
No, but the grub of my bright-winged Redeemer.
(*Plover dashes in, hissing, howling, and in convulsions.*)
    Mrs. S. Hal! Henry! Birdie with you, too? How welcome!
This night of all nights, when the Lord will —
    Dr.   Spirits,
Who breathe out Christian notions, are no tittle
Better than those that frighten fools with hell.
    Mrs. S. Well, when the Lord comes, you will be convinced.
    Dr. Be patient! Is the noblest attribute
Of God not patience? which is one great proof
The Deity is not feminine, my dear.
Just think of the ages — geological! —
Before Creation got its apices
Of Man and this Machine, —
    Mrs. L.   It were much better
For earth, if God were feminine, I think. —
    Dr. And now obstruct not with distrust, or apathy. —
What are you doing Smith Van Doozer?
    Van D. (*With one knee on Plover, having floored him.*)
                                                      Holding
Him during the exorcism.
    Dr.   To ascertain
How the swine felt when they received the legion?
Force after moral suasion, not before it.
By willing master your tormentor, General.
Each man has such a fiend, — this vice, or that, —

Of which he must be master, or a carcass,
Trampled and bloody, on its bison horn.
   Mrs. W. Aleck! my Aleck!
   Dr.   Wait a moment, madam. —
Thou pirate, tramp, in Willard's form, depart.
   Patsy. Divil the foot.
   Dr.   Be good, now; go. Your name,
Friend?
   Patsy.   Patsy I was christened, and begarrah,
Paid well for it, though since, like your redeemer,
I ind in hell, —
   Dr.   Ha!
   Mrs. W.   Oh! —
   Patsy.   'Twas no great bargain.
   Mrs. W. Come, — my poor husband!
   Dr. (*To Mrs. S.*)   Pacify her, dear.
(*To Patsy.*) Where are you from?
   Patsy. (*Changing brogue.*)   From Cork.
   Mrs. W. (*Restrained by Ralph and Mrs. S.*) Oh!
   Dr.   Whence in spirit?
   Patsy. Phew! from the bottom of the bottle — hell.
   Dr. I thought so! In the place called, on account
Of famine in your vocabulary, hell,
Because of drunkardness?
   Patsy.   Have ye the power
Of absolution?
   Dr.   No.
   Patsy.   Why thin confess?
   Dr. When you declare you are in hell, you show
Convincingly that you have been a drunkard,
And have not cast the horrors over your head
Yet, as black snake his skin; hence, when you fleer
At my Messiah, I know I am in Bedlam —
Or ought to be.
   Patsy.   You're right.
   Mrs. W.   Am I unfit
To nurse him?

Dr. Patience! there will be no need
Of nursing, ma'am.
Mrs. W. (*Piteously.*) George!
Col. (*Sharply.*) What?
Dr. Iconoclastic
Spirit, that vultures, sharks, each glorious Movement,
Depart hence, fly, or sink.
Patsy. Faix, I likes company,
I might as well wait for your — phat — is — it?
Dr. Avaunt! Or I shall steep you to the neck
In agony a million years.
Lilla. O, doctor!
Patsy. Phew! be so heartless, cruel?
Dr. Instantly off!
One, two — shall I count three?
Patsy. Oh! at the thought
I melt like vapor on a frosty day
Out of his mouth. (*Plover falls.*)
Dr. (*Whispering to Lilla.*) Be not alarmed, my dear,
About the million years. We banish ignorant
Spirits by threatening them.*
Plover. (*Rising and staggering.*) Gosh! I am under
The ice just long enough.
Col. Doctor, the rite now.
Mrs. W. What! push our Emma's memory out of
    doors
Into the trembling, wet, blue-lipping cold,
To whine, like wind, forever round the house?
Aleck, what does this mean? what does this mean?
These people will vacate my house this instant.
Mrs. S. Did not your darling say, "Heal papa's brow"?
Ralph. Was not your first wife, General, a wild boa
Constrictor that, in a guardless hour, wound round you?
Plover. You bet!
Ralph. Hence, with sky-splitting thunder, Nature
Shrieks, it was never a marriage.

---
* See the letter of the old man to A. J. Davis, in *The Diakka and their Earthly Victims.*

Mrs. W.   Never! — Yet —
Ralph. "What! could I suffer the marshy snake to drag
My eagle down, that lightning-clawed with battle
A nation Heavenward"?
   Plover.   How my head aches, bleeds!
   Dr. Sore for a while is the head with horns wrenched
      off,
But the redeemer will soon heal all sores.
   Patsy. (*Appearing in bishop's robes.*)
By good Saint Patrick, who evicted the shnakes —
Oh! what a pity 'tis that landlords were
Not crapin', thin! — I was here at tin sharp,
To kill off separation, double-fanged
Sarpent, that lies between ye, bites ye both.
   Lilla. Keats! I behold thee, lowering from pink cloud,
In waterfalls of flight, like yellow-birds
Upon bright, breezy mornings, when, alone,
I wandered, like a brooklet, through the meadows,
Becoming a freshet — Mississippi rise —
Of ecstasy with fusing of the glaciers,
Mountains, trees, boulders, birds, streams, towns, and
      hopes.
   Patsy. Will Alexander Willard take for wife
Jane Guilderbury?
   Col. (*To Mrs. W.*)   Humor —
   Mrs. W.   Oh!
   Plover.   I will.
   Patsy. Will you, Jane Guilderbury. —
   Mrs. W.   Willard! Willard! —
   Col. Blame no one but yourself for a relapse —
   Patsy. Have Alexander Willard for your husband?
   Mrs. W. I will.   (*Matilda enters, falling.*)
   Patsy.   I put the ring, eternity,
Not on your finger but around your lives.
Now ye are one, and may ye be a dozen.
   Lilla. How I have thirsted, Cupid, for thy coming!
   Mrs. L. Confound it, blind, old, backing ox, turn
      round,

And see where you are treading.
(*Plover, having been purposely pushed against her by Matilda, sneaks off.*)
    Matilda.   Where am I?
In Pandemonium? Help!
    Mrs. L.   How dare you come
Here, after striving your best to keep back Lilla? —
You powdered, Chinese-footed, jealous thing!
    Matilda. Help! why was I lugged hither by a spirit?
My ears now feel as long as that *old hare's*.
    Mrs. L. I would not want to hang since you were thirty,
My skin might been a drum-head for Bull-Run.
    Matilda. Where — where am I?
    Dr.   At Sister Willard's.
    Matilda.   Sister! —
Pshaw! she that slammed the door right through my bones,
As though I were a dog that had just drawn
Her blood, or roast beef from the table, oven? —
    Ralph. (*To Matilda.*) The meteorite must not fall into a marsh. —
    Matilda. That, missing her husband's heart, called me the thief?
Was it in pocket, or with rouge in the drawer?
A sensible woman would have had it bosomed
Out of the reach of thieves. — What stupid thing
Is floundering there? like lobster in a pot.
    Col. Free, free me! Why the devil don't you wrench
Her neck off?
    Mrs. W. Oh!
    Matilda. (*To Mrs. W.*) Come to the Nugget House,
Where father and Fouracres are now crackling
Their glasses with delight at their escape. —
    Plover (*Grasping Matilda.*) You promised to keep quiet —
    Matilda. (*Eluding him.*)   If you called
Me just before the marriage.
    Plover.   Cracked.

Matilda.   I will
Be more so.
   Plover. (*Seizing her.*) Will you?
   Matilda.   *Oh!* Oh!
   Col. (*Muttering.*)   Smother her.
   Matilda. Off! how dare you be so familiar?
   Mrs. W.   God!
   Matilda. (*Released.*) I spurned you from the first, you
     hateful spider!
That winds around poor, insect-hearted women
So silkenly. (*Flaunts her dress — the purple.*)
   Mrs. W. What! Aleck, do you put
This creature of the street on the scales with me?
Lord!
   Ralph. (*Pushing Matilda.*) Women, when adepts at
     vitrol throwing, —
   Matilda, Could I have held Fouracres to be mur-
     dered? —
   Ralph. Lose right of sanctuary in their sex, —
   Matilda. When Willard, thirsty, followed out the win-
     dow —
Got too stuck up to notice an old neighbor. —
   Ralph. Are dragged out, made to swallow what they
     throw.
   Mrs. W. His father comes. O God! how can I hide
All? Must I share my grief, like wedding-cake,
With friends? 'Tis not. Would that it were! Dear
     Emma!
If here now, speak, direct. A saturnalia
Indeed, — Oh, everywhere! if agonies
Awaken faculties for Heaven in us,
Pinions that have not spreading room on earth,
God! let me fly, let Emma guide from this
Thick fog. — My darling, did you say, " Bear up"?
I will.   [*Exit.*]
   Plover. Say, Colonel! Colonel!
   Lilla. (*Rising toward Cag.*)   Sweetest poet,
Ever thine, wholly! Like the thrilling throat

Of a canary, throb my heart and brain
With melody of love for thee, thee only, —
Love, myriad-noted as the rain of May
On meads, which echo it with odorous flowers, —
As they have throbbed with joy since first I read, —
"A thing of beauty is a joy forever;" —
 Plover. He drained this vial, — leaves me in a hell of
a fix.
Raymond, a lift. He could not brass it out. —
    (*They carry the Col. out.*)
 Lilla. "Its loveliness increases; it will never
Pass into noth" — (*Clasps him.*)   Oh, the blue, welkin-
  ward
Abandon of love, true love, who lets the world
Drop from her raptured fingers!
 Cag. (*Ascending with Lilla in his embrace.*)
       Heavenward! Heavenward!
Aye, like the odorous soul of Flora, when,
Dazzled out of her sleep by the rain, which Earth
Is ever fountaining, like a million whales,
She, tossing her green arms from her all-hued eyes,
Runs up the mountain, leaps the rock, climbs tree,
In passionate pursuit of the lark, her playmate
Amid the dews and grasses.
 Lilla.   Thou, my lark!
 Cag. Back with THE FIRE we come, with Suns re-
  splendent
From beak, — Suns for the heart and mind now moping,
All cold, — as from the beak of bold Columbus,
Scarlet-wing'd, diving bird, this continent
Of golden mountains, meteoric streams,
And nights of forests, northern-lighted with birds.
(*At their touch the machine goes off, emitting showers of
  varied brilliancy. There is great ringing of bells,
  music, and thunderous noises; but all cease sudden-
  ly, and Caglivstro, letting Lilla drop, disappears.*)
 Mrs. S. Lord!

Patsy.   Ha! ha!
Dr.   When will mockers cease tormenting
Mankind?
Patsy.   They are the shadows of the long-nosed
And hump-back world upon the spirit-wall.
    (*Van D. rushes to Lilla, and carries her to the window,
       whose curtains flying up, and shutters out, let in
       the blaze of the forest.*)
Patsy. Phew! my eyes, gouty with high living, ache,
Like jumping teeth, when touched by light.
    (*Smashes the redeemer and disappears.*)
Mrs. L.   Is that
My Lilla?
Matilda.   You have murdered her by letting
Them bring her here.
Mrs. L.   Lilla, my love! O Lilla!
Dead? dead? my Lilla?
Dr.   God! must Reason, noble,
Old Saturn, still have "realmless eyes," starve on?
Still suck the blood of his pale arm for nectar?
Mrs. L. (*Stooping over.*) Lilla, speak, speak! — your
      mother, — speak!
Van D. (*Having closed Lilla's mouth and eyes, and
      having kissed her.*)   Too late!
The gate is closed forever.
Mrs. L. (*Falling on Lilla, and sobbing violently.*)
                         God! Oh! Oh!
Van D. Creation *is* unpillared, it is falling
Before my eyes as miserable, Lilla,
Now that your smile forever is departed.
Could I be sure your spirit, not a mocking
Diakka, would respond, bright were my future,
But no such blessed certitude for me.*
I will embalm you, mummy you, — though wherefore?
That, in a thousand years hence, as rich Greeks,

---

* Professor Wallace says that Spiritualists know well that absolute dependence is to be placed on no individual communication. If on no individual communication, can the logical mind depend on any?

Brothers of Alcibiades, by us
Are, you may be imported for manure
By the New Zealander?
 Mrs. S.   No, dearest Lord,
We need not droop our heads, give way to tears.
Thou, *Wisest!* wert no fool to promise what
Thou never couldst perform. What! Purity's self
A heinous, villanous impostor? Could
The Sun shine black? congeal the earth? — The Sun
That, like an urchin, with long, golden curls,
Bending above the lake with crumbling cake,
Attracts shoal after shoal of verdure, fruit,
And flowers, white, purple, crimson, to the surface?
No. As this evening Thou didst reaffirm,
Thou wilt come, nor be as a passing breeze,
Which lets our feverish heads blaze up again.
I beg Thee, only say that Lilla liveth.
 Dr. Fool! fool! to have believed the rainbow would
Be rounded on earth, — be more the bow of God,
Springing out after arrowing the Deluge,
Now, than when Noah's black ark was fastened among
The arctic ice-bergs of the ghastly dead!
 Ralph. (*Entering.*) A comet may strike earth, etherealize it
Without, as with an angry whale's tail, tossing
It sky-high, like a yawl, or life-boat.
 Mrs. L.   This
The trailing silks of glory?
 Ralph.   It may pass
Through earth, nor less effectual, unperceived.
 Dr. I am no Millerite to swallow that.
No higher can man, with hunger still more maddening,
Progress. Is it his destiny to craze?
 Mrs. L. My darling! this the opening of my eyes?
 Ralph. (*Whispering.*) Tillie, my love, come.
 Matilda.   I mistrust the dog
That, after snapping, licks my face, — there is
Saliva in him.

Ralph. To the devil with you,
Then. If the Colonel should revive, beware.
(*Whispering.*) Thief!
  Matilda. I have worn it, I am satisfied,
Shall throw it to her and un-throat all, all!
Fetch Sarah Plover here this very night. —
    (*Goes to Mrs. L.*)
Dear Sister Lamb, if I can be of service
To you in any way, do mention it.
  Mrs. L. Lilla, my darling! Am I never more
To see your face, so beautiful that even
Old, envious Sarah Plover called you lovely?
Oh! Never more to comb your golden hair
Down to your graceful swan-neck of a waist,
The envy of all mothers and their girls. (*Sobs.*)
  Van D. (*With hand on Mrs. L's shoulder.*)
Try to restrain.
  Mrs. L. Oh! you have lost no daughter.
  Van D. Dear Sister Lamb, keen is your anguish, but
No, no, not more than mine. Her dreamy, large,
Blue eyes, by her tiny left hand shaded from
The Sun-light, springing suddenly, as squirrel,
Upon her from the trees, surprising her
So that she staggers and upsets her bloomer
Of choicest flowers, — Oh! such a sight no more;
It lifted creation from the eely mud
Of rueful musing; but no more! no more!
  Dr. Father Almighty! is it dark despair,
The vortical shadow of the earth gyrating,
Like a tornado, up to Thee, wherein
He now must plunge? There, plunging head-long down,
I hear him bellow, — "Oh! I was Thy dog,
To whom Thou flungest what was sweetest, grandest,
Earth, sun, sea, seasons, music, law, and beauty,
That in the end Thou, like a cruel wretch," —
  Mrs S. Oh! Oh! because God does not fall, surren-
    der
To your vagary unconditionally. —

Dr. " Mayst pour down into my swift-swallowing throat
An iron, glowing white and soft as milk,
The hope of meeting Thee yet, face to face." —
    Van D. We must not be splashed backward, Squig-
        ginson,
But manfully overswim the deluge, pouring
On us from all horizons, though we land
Just *nowhere*, nowhere. To phenomenal
Nature, some, with the poet, rush from grief,
And others, with the mystic, seek the Soul.
I have sought both; in each have found a wolf
With eyes and teeth set glistening, under which
I could not think to lay me down to rest.
Oh! we know nothing but *excruciation!*
Which Jesus, recognizing, glorified
As the grape-arbored way to a Heavenly Mansion.
Action, dear brother, action! Let us blind
Ourselves with action, and with action deaden
The malady of thought, fast-fueling Hell
Of sensibility. Wherein does genius
Itself, Sir, differentiate from madness?*
Expect no Calsium Light behind the world,
The grand procession wherein whooping tribes,
Sky-rocketing nations, hold before their heads
Their theories, creeds, dark, blinding torch-lights! Action!
Action for Man — the first we meet — not that
Vague god, Humanity, — huge Brocken Shadow,
Before whom thousands bow most noble heads,
Swing richest incense, — not one jot superior
To snow-gods, all tattoed with dirt and stone,
Which brawny tribes rolled up their native hills
In Time's dark morning.
    Mrs. L.   This for offering you —
Oh, as a fatherless child! — with these mad arms
To spirits on the night I meant to hang
Myself? (*Sobs.*)

---

    * A few years ago a French physician, of some repute as a medical writer, wrote a treatise to show that genius was a form of dementia.

Mrs. S. (*Lifting Lilla's head.*)
                    Command her to arise, and, Lord!
Do straighten the sight of those who turn their eyes
Into their sockets to their will from Thine.
   Dr. God! laugh Thy fill now at my rolling, plunging,
And paw-disboweling.
   Mrs. L. (*Rushing at Dr.*) Give me back my darling, —
You told me what she said was true! was true! —
Must have her! Give me back my Lilla, ever
My warm heart — at my side — a heart that never
Could fail me! *Give me back my darling child!*
   Dr. (*Eluding her.*)
Let out annihilation from Thy heart,
Thy all eternity-harbored " ha! ha! ha! "
   Mrs. S. Lord God! dost Thou in this dark hour forsake me?
Pity us all. — Do I ask Thee to pity?
All human pity for our kind that ever
Could be, were but a dew-drop on a daisy,
Compared with Thine, which is an endless rain,
A deluge, though unseen by us, poor fools,
Who fancy that our hearts are larger than Thine,
And with this fancy so afflict our souls.
   (*Cagliostro reappears amid clouds.*)
Welcome, O dearest Lord! Oh! welcome, welcome!
Once that this Babel lay demolished, as
All such must lie, I was as sure of seeing
Thee, as if I had just approached the Mount
Where thousands, quiet as a snowy morn,
Stood, and from clay changed into violets,
Lillies, and roses, an oasis sweet
To angels deserting since Eden sank,
Beneath Thy zephyr voice. O Thou, who breathest
On wintry earth, and it is Spring! I beg Thee,
Behold poor Lilla. With Thy garment's hem
Only just touch her! touch my husband, too, —
Oh! all the world, which is to be the more
Pitied because, like owls, it hoots at light,

At those who mean well, — even those far astray —
Oh! even, Lord, those who, having lost Thy trail,
Follow the moon, their promptings, round and round
The prairies, and lie hopeless down, thirst, craze,
Deny that there is water, or an East.
    Mrs. L. Lilla, my darling ! — give me back my Lilla !
With heart as large as her golden hair was long. —
Oh! must that hair, you had no patience to rack,
And were so proud of, grow now in the grave
Neglected ? like the yellow weeds, — " on which
The black-winged shiner feeds, but does not sing,
For he soars chirping to the cedar-peak,
As may my spirit from weedy earth to God." —
Amen! amen! my darling child, amen!
    Mrs. W. (*Running in and falling, followed by the Judge with a glittering bayonet.*) God! (*Cag., disappearing slowly, fixes his gaze on the Judge.*)
    Judge.   His will —
    Mrs. W.   George! George!
    Judge. (*Feeling for her heart.*) And not mine, dear child.
One second, dear.
    Matilda. (*Springing in between Mrs. W. and the Judge.*)   God! save her! — Oh!
(*Matilda is pierced through the breast, and the Judge is disarmed and restrained by Van D.*)
    Judge.   Earth, tossed
By stormy-headed winter in the air,
Is falling down on the bison's horn, to be
All gored, nay, trampled on, hurled upward again.
    Matilda. (*Staggering.*) Maybe she will believe me now, her sister. (*Drops.*)
    Judge. Jane, fly! thou art the angel to catch the world,
Hug it to breast, as were it Emma found,
And stand on the beast till it, exhausted, drops.
To hold thee would make me a *damned* abettor,
    Jane. I am no abettor ! (*To Van D.*) Off thou fury
Of hell! ferocious imprecation from

My own child's mouth, off! off! Infernal harpy!
Thou shalt not stench my daily bread; shalt not
Claw off my hope of Heaven when I am dying.
   Dr. With strength developed, I WILL conquer all.
   Judge. Oh! horrible beyond all utterance — horrible! —
   Dr. Woe to the circling hawk that dares approach,
Or moon-struck woman, — woman with heart-pearled
    eyes.—   [*Exit.*]
   Judge Must that Last Supper be where Christ is not.
But He will be at mine, since I am not
A damned abettor; for I set her free
To snatch our Land up from the mutilation
Of savages, and blazing of forest, prairie,
Village, and city, universal ruin,
That would have followed glorious Willard's downfall.
   Mrs. S. Like furious billows, horrors splash upon me,
O Lord! but I walk over them to Thee,
With firmer step than up a hill of granite
" To the Sun-mitred East, before whom Ocean
Marches sublimely with his acolytes
Of waves, each genuflecting reverently
To earth, peak-lighted altar, choired by birds,
Incensed by swinging forests, and Thy Foot-stool,
God! Good! Eternal Beauty"! — In Thy name
(*Trembling*), I say, — Matilda! be thou healed; walk
    forth;
And Lilla! rise. I say, ARISE! WALK FORTH!
    (*She lifts Lilla's hand. After a pause Mrs. L.
    breaks out afresh. Van D. struggles with the
    Judge, and gorgeous are the clouds after Cagliostro's set.*)

www.ingramcontent.com/pod-product-compliance
Lightning Source LLC
Chambersburg PA
CBHW031335160426
43196CB00007B/694